STALEBREAD
and the RAZZY DAZZY SPASM BAND

An Origin Story of Jazz in New Orleans

Michael Shurtz

Genius
Music Books

Milwaukee Wisconsin USA

Stalebread and the Razzy Dazzy Spasm Band

Copyright © 2026 Michael Shurtz

Published by:
Genius Book Publishing
PO Box 250380
Milwaukee Wisconsin 53225 USA
GeniusBookPublishing.com

Cover image courtesy of the Hogan Archive of New Orleans Music and New Orleans Jazz.

ISBN: 978-1-958727-88-1

251123 HQ

Contents

ACKNOWLEDGMENTS

My editor, Nile Southern; the Hogan Archive of New Orleans Music and New Orleans Jazz, specifically curator emeritus Bruce Boyd Raeburn and archivists Kure Croker, Ann Case, Agnes Czeblakow, Mallisa Webber, and Alaina Hebert; the William Ransom Hogan Jazz Archive; the Al Rose Collection, the Monroe Library Special Collections at Loyola University; the Louisiana Historical Society; New Orleans Jazz Museum curator Greg Lambousy, and curator emeritus Don Marquis; Tim Benko; Dan Reina; and Risë Keller; with special thanks to Susan Schulman of Susan Schulman Literary Agency, and Leya and Steven Booth of Genius Book Publishing.

Cover photo: From left to right, Warm Gravy, Stalebread, Chinee, Monk, Family Haircut, Cajun. Taken at the Chas. Tyemi Studio, New Orleans, Louisiana, c. 1897.

To my daughter Emily and my son Kyle
In memory of Rose Lacoume Weaver

The members of the Razzy Dazzy Spasm Band, who serenaded all and sundry on District banquettes, were a noteworthy collection. Perhaps the most celebrated was Emile "Stalebread" Lacoume, considered by some to be the first jazz musician.

—Al Rose, from *Storyville, New Orleans: Being an Authentic, Illustrated Account of the Notorious Red Light District*

INTRODUCTION: THE ORIGINAL BOY BAND

This is the tale of New Orleans' least-known pioneer of jazz. In 1988, I first came across the studio portrait of The Razzy Dazzy Spasm Band in the book *New Orleans, A Pictorial History,* by Leonard V. Huber. The remarkable photograph, taken at Chas. Tyemi's Studio on Canal Street in the 1890s, captivated my curiosity for a number of reasons, not least of which was the boys' confident pose. This formal portrait meant business, it seemed to me. There was not much accompanying the picture, but the author mentioned another book, *Storyville, New Orleans,* by Al Rose. I bought a copy of Rose's book, and lo and behold, the same photo appeared with a paragraph naming the members of the band. This further piqued my interest, but left me with more questions than answers. I hoped to find a biography, but found none.

The only book I found was a children's book about Stalebread and his associates called *Stalebread Charlie and the Razzy Dazzy Spasm Band,* written by Michael Mahin and illustrated by Don Tate. In my research I found that

Emile "Stalebread" Lacoume never had a "Charlie" in his name. This moniker was invented by a Catholic priest from up north who was doing some colorful journalism while visiting New Orleans around 1900. He wrote a piece about the newsboys in New Orleans that dubbed him "Stalebread Charlie."

My research began before the advent of the Internet, so at first, I relied solely on the Library of Congress' Dewey Decimal System resources. To my disappointment, I found nothing else on the subjects of Emile "Stalebread" Lacoume or The Razzy Dazzy Spasm Band. I had to wait over a decade for the arrival of search engines to deepen my research.

My tale of Emile "Stalebread" Lacoume is a hybrid of historical fiction and biography. I have retold verbatim and paraphrased stories Lacoume told to journalists. Also, I include second-hand accounts and details shared by his wife, his daughter, historians, and other contributors. Lastly, I invented some dialogue and fictional passages to fill out the legends and lore I turned up in my research.

While visiting New Orleans in the summer of 1990, I went to the Musée Conti Wax Museum in the French Quarter to see their life-sized diorama of Stalebread and his band. The now-defunct museum was housed in an eighteenth-century Spanish Colonial building on Conti Street. At different times, the building had contained a boys' school, an oyster saloon, a coffee shop, a coffin factory, and a textile sweatshop.

The Musée Conti's labyrinthine passageways were illuminated by the lighting of the dioramas populated by wax figures portraying pivotal moments in New Orleans' history. According to a paranormal team's overnight investigations, the building also counted at least three ghosts among its residents.

Of the museum's many dioramas, four were dedicated to local jazz legends: Ferdinand Joseph La Menthe, aka "Jelly Roll" Morton, Louis "Satchmo" Armstrong, clarinetist Pete Fountain, and Emile "Stalebread" Lacoume (accompanied by two members of The Razzy Dazzy Spasm Band). In their diorama, the boys played their homemade instruments and sang next to a prostitute's shanty. A red lantern hung by the door, casting its crimson glow onto a pair of prostitutes frozen in a hair-pulling brawl. It impressed me that Stalebread and his Razzy Dazzy Spasm Band were considered important enough to be given their own diorama alongside revered jazz musicians Armstrong, Morton, and Fountain.

During this period, I had no intention of writing a book on Stalebread, but I was gathering the stories that would eventually become the backbone of this book. One story that David Kunian, the music curator of the New Orleans Jazz Museum, directed me to was an invaluable article by Jack Stewart, "The Mexican Band Legend: Myth, Reality, and Musical Impact," that appeared in the newsletter of the Tulane University Hogan Archive of New Orleans Music and New Orleans Jazz. Stewart's article describes the Mexican influence on New Orleans music in the late 19th century and how Stalebread and other New Orleans musicians fell under the spell of this musical trend.

While researching what life was like for these kids, I thought about the effects of running around barefoot in the largest city in the South, and the different cultural attitudes and practices between the 1890s and now. For instance, cigarettes, cigars, and pipes were ubiquitous and the aroma of tobacco smoke was everywhere, even in the few places where people did not smoke. Its smell clung to everyone's clothes. Not only was society promiscuous about the habit of smoking, but it was also indifferent to the age of a child who might fall into the habit. It was as common to see a cigarette dangling from a boy's lips as it was a rope of licorice. Of course, more conscientious adults would have lectured children about the evils of smoking, but even they would stop scolding children over about the age of six. By then the boys would have given in to peer pressure, curiosity, habit, addiction, or all of the above. If a kid had never smoked before, he would most likely start soon after joining a group of smokers.

The strict enforcement of Jim Crow laws had a strong influence during the formative years of jazz music. After decades of the laws being relatively relaxed, in the 1890s, they were once again being strictly enforced in New Orleans. As was the case throughout the South, music was no exception to the Jim Crow laws because music constituted "socializing." Consequently, two parallel branches of jazz forked from the genre's inception: black and white. It would be decades before legal barriers were removed and these boundaries were dissolved. Meanwhile, regardless of the imposed segregation, musicians from both branches were looking over each other's shoulders, and listening and learning from one another.

Both black and white musicians were exploring the rhythms of *habanera* music. Habanera music originated in

Havana, Cuba, and has African and European influences. It spread from Cuba in the 19th century. One example of habanera's many migrations was to Mexico, where habanera developed its own national flavor. The Mexican habanera beat was first introduced to the United States in 1884, in the city of New Orleans.

The Spanish tinge (or "Latin Tinge") is an essential ingredient in the entire variety of habanera. While it originated in Havana, many nations have their own flavors of habanera: Spain, Puerto Rico, Brazil, and Mexico. Like dialects, each region had its own style. The word "Tinge" refers to the syncopation accentuating the up beat that provides the provocative lilt in their rhythms. These syncopated accents are said to give off the sensation of heat. "Hot" was an apt term for the North American style of habanera and it was called hot in the United States before the term "jazz" was invented.

An in-depth understanding of The Spanish tinge can be had from reading John Storm Robert's excellent book *The Latin Tinge*. You can also find very good YouTube videos on the subject. One of my favorites is a four-minute audio recording of Jelly Roll Morton mentioning the Spanish tinge.

"Jass" was another word that entered the vernacular, but this was a slur lobbed by white journalists denigrating Black musicians who played hot music. The word "jass" was coined by a New Orleans society page columnist whose pretentious editorial column regarded the new music with contempt. His commentaries were often accompanied by racist cartoons depicting black musicians blasting a cacophony of noise that repelled white socialites.

The spelling eventually morphed from "jass" into "jazz."' I provide a deeper explanation of this later in this book.

In researching Stalebread, one of my most memorable encounters was with George Buck Jr., the blind discographer and jazz preservationist who lived in New Orleans. George once owned a number of radio stations along the eastern seaboard and had amassed the largest collection of traditional jazz records in the world. His encyclopedic knowledge of traditional jazz was not only in his memory but also at his fingertips as he flipped through his braille Rolodex. George's record collection occupied the top floor of an old warehouse on Decatur Street in the French Quarter. His wife Nina owned the small jazz haven The Palm Court Cafe below him on the ground floor.

I came to George to learn whether there were any Stalebread recordings, or credits attributed to him. George combed through his file cabinet, searching for evidence in recording logs and liner notes. George could not find anything of this sort. Despite coming up empty-handed, it was a pleasure spending time with George in his French Quarter loft, searching for any trace of Stalebread.

Edmund "Doc" Souchon's 1961 interview with Stalebread's widow, Annie, revealed that Annie used to beg him to record. Stalebread had certainly had plenty of opportunities.

Stalebread's wife, Annie

Some musicians resist being recorded for fear of having their secrets revealed and stolen. Some musicians have regular jobs and families, and beyond playing music with friends at parties, have neither the time nor the energy to record. Some musicians are fearful of being ostracized by fundamentalist family members who consider their genre "the devil's music." These musicians choose to record under pseudonyms. As with Buddy Bolden, Stalebread, and many others, it's unfortunate that they didn't get recorded.

Another individual I became acquainted with was historian and author Al Rose. He is best remembered for his 1974 historic exposé *Storyville, New Orleans: Being an Authentic, Illustrated Account of the Notorious Red Light District.* (This book that inspired and informed director Louis Malle's movie *Pretty Baby.*) Al Rose was a New Orleans historian, and a traditional jazz historian. He encouraged me in my research of Stalebread, insisting the Razzy Dazzy Spasm Band was the first professional "hot band" to play jazz in the District (later known as Storyville). At the time Stalebread got his hot band together, several local professional and amateur bands were transitioning into hot bands. This is a key distinction between The Razzy Dazzy Spasm Band and other contemporary bands. Those professional bands were paid to play, and their repertoires didn't include hot music at first. About The Razzy Dazzy Spasm Band, however, Stalebread used to say, "Never been nothin' but hot!"

Some historians did not take The Razzy Dazzy Spasm Band seriously. Fredrick Ramsey Jr., a 24-year-old Princeton grad, and his co-author Charles Edward Smith, a 35-year-old Connecticut-based record collector, were discographers writing for jazz periodicals when they published *Jazzmen* in 1939. Their book sold well because it was the first book dedicated to the new academic subject of jazz history. They were dismissive of Stalebread and his band. The authors erroneously asserted that The Razzy Dazzy Spasm Band only played professionally once they had "legitimate musical instruments." On the contrary, the band always played both factory-made instruments and homemade instruments, and they were grateful to have whichever they could get their hands on.

The Razzy Dazzy Spasm Band began playing hot music for a living long before the Victrola record player was introduced in 1906. By 1939, popular mainstream jazz had become polished almost beyond recognition, with Paul Whiteman's symphonic orchestra considered the epitome of sophisticated jazz. The purveyors of popular music, Walt Disney among them, hailed Whiteman as the latest "King of Jazz." (Dubbing musicians "King" goes back to the reign of cornetist Buddy "King" Bolden, who was possibly the first to be so crowned. His protege Joe "King" Oliver, a mentor of Louis Armstrong, inherited the crown from Buddy Bolden.)

While on a tour stop in New Orleans, Paul Whiteman sought out Stalebread and the two met. Whiteman later told newspaper reporters he had wanted to meet "the father of jazz music."

Spasm hadn't changed over the ensuing decades, but jazz steadily became more refined as it went forward. Consequently, the old-fashioned rag-tag Razzy Dazzy Spasm Band received scant attention in *Jazzmen*. The Ivy

League-educated authors chided, "A lot of nonsense has been talked about Stalebread and his Spasm Band. Jazz didn't come from toy instruments, no matter how quaint or colorful these street corner bands sound to the tourist trade."

The Razzy Dazzy Spasm Band had Chris Nielsen to thank for their homemade instruments. He was the little carpenter whose workshop was next door to the Newsboys' Home. While researching years ago, I came across this heartwarming interview of Nielsen by T. D. Wharton, published in 1923 in the Freemasons' Louisiana Lodge Light newsletter, headlined "Brother Chris and Jazz."

Chris Nielsen: If it be true that "Jazz" music had its origin in New Orleans through the "instrumentality" of the newsboys' crude band headed by "Stalebread," the famous newsboy of thirty-five years ago, then I had something to do with this momentous event, The latest "nut" song, "Yes, We Have No Bananas" was being mentioned together with many remarkable airs of that class and "jazz" generally.

T.D. Wharton: We all knew the wide range of subjects that came within Brother Nielsen's purview, but admittedly this was a new one on us.

Nielsen: You remember the old Newsboys' Home on Baronne Street near Perdido? Well one day, the priest in charge, Father Nicholas, a Belgian by the way, came to my shop, to see if I could suggest some way to rig-up a few simple things for a little gymnasium he wished to start for the boys. The priest was a man of the world, an attractive and entertaining conversationalist, and in the course of my visits to the Home, he and I became very friendly. During these visits I had occasion to meet many of the newsboys. Whenever Father Nicholas looked toward my shop and saw I was not busy, he would come over and smoke a pipe with me, and the subject of talks included philosophy, religion, art, music and anything else that happened to attract our attention. In this way, I got to be very familiar with the Home and the boys.

One day Stalebread and several others came to me to see if I could make a bass fiddle out of a small barrel they brought along. They explained they were getting up a band composed of harmonicas, paper and combs, improvised violins, etc. and they needed this bass fiddle to complete the equipment. Well, I was glad to help in this musical enterprise and I succeeded in making out of the barrel an instrument that they pronounced "bully."

As I recall it, there were four or five in their band and they would stand on St. Charles or Royal Streets at night and play on these originally designed instruments, followed of course by a collection from passers-by. They would take a popular air of the day and give it that peculiar rhythm, or lack of rhythm you might say, that twist which has been perfected in the "nut" music of the present day. I suppose the idea was half original and half borrowed from the strange sounds that certain negroes gave in their voodoo dances back of town, as well as the hootchie coochie airs that came from the midway at the World's Fair in Chicago. This band of Stalebread's became famous and it has been claimed that they are responsible for Jazz.

Nielsen: You remember the smoker Louisiana gave at the Grunewald Hotel just before prohibition when we buried John Barleycorn? Well, one of the players in the orchestra that night, I learned during the evening, was Stalebread. He was a stout man of middle age and totally blind. I shook hands with him and recalled the incident of the bass fiddle. I thought he would never let go of my hand. "So, you are the little carpenter that helped us out. I sure am glad to see you." Up to then I had thought he was dead.

Wharton: "Jazz" might have come to us anyhow, even without the barrel bass fiddle, but history demands that the part Chris played in the introduction of this renowned class of music shall be duly recorded.

As for the sound of these instruments, their volume improved when they played under the tin roofs of the train sheds or the canvas awnings stretched over sidewalks. Family Haircut used a stovepipe to amplify his paper-and-comb. Microphones were introduced in the late 1890s, so there is the possibility Stalebread and his band would have used them if they could have. I have no doubt the boys would have loved the electric microphone. With their proclivity for invention, I can just imagine them discovering feedback and putting it to "good trouble," the way Jimi Hendrix did decades later.

Over the years, handcrafted cigar-box guitars have gained so much in popularity worldwide that cigar-box guitar festivals have popped up around the world. One of these is the New Orleans Cigar Box Guitar Festival, held every January at the venerable New Orleans Jazz Museum. These days, the overwhelming majority of cigar-box guitars are electric, outfitted with pickups and an amplifier. The Festival presents a cash prize award for the best acoustic cigar-box guitar, called "The Razzy Dazzy Award," in honor of Chris Nielsen's legacy, and to encourage luthiers to carry on the tradition of their less popular old-school acoustic forerunners. Whether acoustic or electric, cigar-box luthiers love the opportunity to build fantastic one-off stringed instruments that surprise and delight.

Until the "British Invasion" of the 1960s, when the Beatles and other English bands dominated the charts in the U.S., American folk, jazz, rhythm and blues, and country and western music were popular with English audiences. America's "spasm" music is cited as an influence in English "roots" music, skiffle. Spasm's primitive charm must have been a liberating ingredient. As with spasm, skiffle gave old songs new life by deranging, rearranging, and discombobulating them.

Another similarity skiffle bands shared with spasm bands was their use of homemade instruments. The reason The Razzy Dazzy Spasm Band members made some of their own instruments was simple: they were poor, and factory-made instruments cost money they didn't have to spare. Regardless of their poverty, these boys had a burning desire to play hot music as a band.

Likewise, in war-ravaged England during the post war 1940s, factory-made instruments were expensive; even second-hand instruments were costly. This was because there had been a market shortage of factory-built instruments during and after World War II. In the late 1940s and early 1950s, factories were still retrofitting following their wartime assignments and had not yet returned to pre-war productivity. During this period, there were not enough factory-made instruments in England to meet the burgeoning demand for them. As with Stalebread and his band, necessity was the mother of invention. Eager to play music, the English lads resorted to making their own stringed instruments. Like the Razzy Dazzy Spasm Band, they played whatever they had, whether manufactured or homemade.

Many of England's most famous rock-and-roll musicians cut their teeth in working-class skiffle bands like John Lennon's first band The Quarrymen, in which a washtub, a broom handle, and a clothesline stood in for a bass fiddle. Irishman Lonnie Donegan, a banjo player for English traditional jazz bandleader Chris Barber, left Barber's band and went on his own to play skiffle. Lonnie scored a hit skiffle record with Leadbelly's "Rock Island Line." He soon was crowned—you guessed it—the "King of Skiffle." The Lonnie Donegan Skiffle Group sported a corrugated washboard scrubbed to the rhythm of their washtub bass. Lonnie inspired legions of young men to start bands and play whatever instruments they had. Many of the old songs that skiffle bands played had their origins in the days of the English broadsides; The Razzy Dazzy Spasm Band once played some of these songs, too.

Another influential English traditional jazz musician was singer-songwriter-guitarist Alexis Korner, who played in Ken Colyer's skiffle group. Alexis also played for jazzman Chris Barber at The Marquee Club on London's Oxford Street. It's said that during Barber's intermissions, Alexis and harmonica player-vocalist Cyril Davies started playing blues-infused skiffle. Their concoction was an instant hit with Barber's audiences. Soon Alexis and Cyril formed a side group that they named Blues Incorporated. Blues Incorporated became a fertile breeding ground for early British blues musicians. The Marquee is recognized as the original hot spot of the British blues scene. Alexis' and Cyril Davies' Blues Incorporated group included Dick Heckstall-Smith on sax, Jack Bruce on bass, Charlie Watts (of The Rolling Stones fame) on drums, and lead singer Long John Baldry from the Bob Cort Skiffle Group. Alexis Korner mentored many younger musicians, including Brian Jones (The Rolling Stones) and John Paul Jones (Led Zeppelin). Other famous English skiffle alumni include John Lennon, Paul McCartney, Mick Jagger, Ronnie Wood, David Gilmour, Jimmy Page, Graham Nash, just to name a few. A comprehensive account of the skiffle genre can be found in Billy Bragg's excellent book *Roots, Radicals and Rockers: How Skiffle Changed the World*. The Razzy Dazzy Spasm Band in the 1890s and English skiffle bands in the 1950s showed the same pluck and determination.

A pivotal year for my research occurred in 1990, when

I met jazz historian and biographer Donald M. Marquis, the curator of The New Orleans Jazz Museum. Marquis is best known for his definitive biography *In Search of Buddy Bolden, First Man of Jazz*. Marquis told me he knew Stalebread's only daughter, Rose Lacoume Weaver, and offered to call her on my behalf. He asked Rose if she would be willing to speak to me about her father, and she graciously consented.

When I called Rose, I heard the gentle voice of a woman in her early seventies with a proper New Orleans' accent. I was nervous, but Rose's manner put me at ease. We conversed long enough to realize we could talk for hours. Before saying goodbye, Rose invited me to visit her next time I was in New Orleans. When Mardi Gras came around, I flew from Oakland to New Orleans to meet her.

Rose and her husband Peter lived in the West End neighborhood, near Lake Pontchartrain. I brought a notepad, though I did not take many notes, nor did I ask many questions, as my voice was hoarse from shouting for beads during the two previous days of Mardi Gras parades. It was a wonderful visit, sitting around their dining-room table and listening to Stalebread's daughter and son-in-law's reminiscences. The couple recounted Stalebread's idiosyncrasies, pet peeves, and personal traits. I knew Rose's father had gone blind at the age of fifteen, and it was fascinating to hear her recollections of their home life. "Closed doors were forbidden in our house," she said, "and if Daddy ran into one, well, we would hear it and skedaddle."

Peter Weaver and Rose Lacoume Weaver

Rose also shared with me some of Stalebread's survival tactics, such as tying a knot in his fishing line a foot above the hook to avoid the stinging whiskers of the catfish. Her favorite memories were personal ones, such as him bringing her along to high-society house parties in the Garden District, where he was hired as an entertainer. She began accompanying him when she was only four years old. She fondly recalled how he would perch her up on the piano to sing along with him, and it was obvious Rose still adored her father.

Rose told me her parents first met at her aunt's eighteenth birthday party when her mother, Annie, was 15. Her father was 18 at the time. They didn't meet again until Annie was 29. At that time, the attraction was mutual and immediate. Annie's stepfather at first did not approve. He was skeptical that his daughter's blind fiancé could support her. However, after learning that Emile was already a homeowner, had a savings account, and had good credit, Annie's stepfather began to come around. He was also impressed that Stalebread was a devout Catholic who never missed Sunday Mass. Stalebread dressed sharply and was smart about his finances, too, a self-sufficient young man. Stalebread soon put to rest her stepfather's fears about Annie's future. Stalebread would fulfill his lifelong dream of building a custom home: Rose told me, "We had a basement, which was unusual in New Orleans. Only the most modern homes in New Orleans were being built with basements back then."

To my disappointment, Rose did not have any stories to relay from her father's colorful youth. "I don't remember Daddy talking about his childhood," she admitted. Rose had just one sibling, her brother Emile III.

In one of jazz historian Doc Souchon's 1961 audio interviews with Stalebread's widow Annie, I learned that Stalebread had intended to dictate his memoir to a young gentleman from Tulane University in 1946, when Stalebread was 61. As fate would have it, Stalebread died on the day he was supposed to sign the publishing agreement at a lawyer's office.

Despite Rose's lack of stories about her father's childhood, she talked about a very important time in her father's career that I was unaware of. "I know Daddy worked for Lulu White at Mahogany Hall, down on Basin Street. That was a bordello, you know."

I found out that, as an adult, Stalebread had become one of Lulu White's "Professors"—the piano players at her and other bordellos. "Daddy even worked for Lulu after the government shut down The District." In 1917, during World War I, the War Department shut Storyville down because soldiers and sailors on leave were picking up and spreading social diseases in alarming numbers. "Daddy worked for Lulu at her new place after that. He was well into his thirties when Lulu finally retired from the business."

Annie confided to Doc that she lost a few "moralistic" friends who shunned her after learning her husband was employed by the infamous Lulu White. Annie defended her husband:

Emile was making a great income at Mahogany Hall, and he always came straight home from work with his money. I had no reservations about him working for Lulu White, none at all. I never did meet her but Emile said she was an honest person and a good businesswoman. She treated him well, and even paid for his cab ride home every night, so he wouldn't have to walk home by himself. Those gossipy women didn't know my husband. He was a well-respected man about town and had many respectable friends. Everybody wanted to be Emile's friend.

Making music provided Stalebread's income throughout his adulthood. He played piano, banjo, and guitar, and sang with a variety of bands and orchestras. Stalebread also entertained at private parties, accompanying himself on piano. He was a private tutor and had a small studio in the French Quarter, where he charged fifty cents an hour (about $19 today) and hung a sign in the window guaranteeing he would teach you to play banjo in one lesson or you'd get your money back. Being the family breadwinner, he augmented his income by selling the *Daily Racing Form* at the Fair Grounds during the horse-racing season. He was one of a dozen blind vendors at the racetrack who were sponsored by the Lighthouse for the Blind.

Rose told me, "Daddy was friends with a federal judge, and a lot of other important people around town. Stalebread recognized everyone by their voice and greeted them by name. One day, at the race track, the Fair Grounds president walked up to him and said, 'Hello, Emile.' Without missing a beat, he replied, 'How do you do, Mr. Dimond?' The next day in one of the morning papers, there was a write-up about it. People were fascinated by this ability of his.

Photo from 1929 featuring the blind program-sellers who worked the Fair Grounds, including Stalebread, fourth from the left.

Blind vendors selling programs at the Fairgrounds racetrack; Stalebread is fourth from left

"Daddy was also good friends with Harry Blackstone, who he tutored in music," Rose said. The world-famous magician was born just five days after Stalebread in 1885. Blackstone became a professional in his teens and the two of them shared a history of becoming paid entertainers at a young age. According to Annie, they stayed in touch even after Blackstone moved to Los Angeles.

Rose told me about her father's long friendship with the world-famous English stage actress Olga Nethersole: "She was Daddy's guardian angel." Their friendship is an important part of this book.

In 1992, I moved with my family from Oakland, California to Kenner, a suburb of New Orleans. I was a stay-at-home dad with our two- and four-year-old at the time. Rose and one of her daughters once paid me a visit. Rose wanted to see the portrait I was painting of her father. In the painting, Stalebread is hawking a newspaper while surfing on a homemade bass fiddle, in a stadium filled with red peppers. Unconventional as it was, she approved of it, and I was glad it pleased her. Rose's only suggestion was to add print to the newspapers, which I'd yet to do. Of course I honored her suggestion.

Every so often, Rose would call me, or I'd call her just to chat. Around then, Rose asked me to write a book about her father. I was not yet a published author, but I was a writer, illustrator, and cartoonist. At first, I created a *Stalebread* comic; I thought it would be a catchy pitch to the New Orleans *Times-Picayune*: a comic strip in their newspaper about newsboys in Gay Nineties New Orleans who had once hawked their paper. I was pleased with my presentation of one month's worth of daily installments and four large Sunday strips, but my pitch failed to excite *The Times-Picayune's* editors. I was only disappointed that I hadn't been able to fulfill the promise I'd made to Rose. She thought the comic was cute, but it was not what she'd been hoping for.

About a year later, I wrote and illustrated a children's book using Stalebread and the Razzy Dazzy Spasm Band as the main characters. (Mahin and Tate's children's book *Stalebread Charlie* had not yet been published.) In my story, the boys in the band join in adventures with a grizzly bear named Scratch. Scratch is a wild honky-tonk piano star, a veritable Jerry Lee Lewis who destroys every piano he plays by the end of his performances. The Razzy Dazzy Spasm Band were his opening act and they were on the road together in places like Natchez Under-the-Hill, and Lollygag Bend. Every venue provided an obligatory sacrificial piano, and the owners had to buy a replacement. Scratch was a high-maintenance star in that regard, but the concerts always made lots of money whenever Scratch performed at their place. I thought it was a good premise for a children's book, but I knew this was not what Rose had in mind when she asked me to write a book about her father.

I took my children's book illustrations to Disney Studios in Burbank, hoping they would be interested in an adaptation of Stalebread's story. My old friend Ron Clements, animation director at Disney, put me in touch with Charlie Fink, then vice president for creative affairs. Fink politely listened to my pitch, and good-naturedly let me know Disney wasn't interested. I was surprised until I learned much later that at this time, Disney was in preproduction with their live-action musical *Newsies* (which takes place in New York City in the 1890s). Charlie Fink must've thought I was daft for pitching another turn-of-the-century musical newsboys movie to them.

A few years later, I was on the lookout for the best place to bequeath my research papers as I didn't feel ready to write a full-length book. I approached Ken Burns' Florentine Films, as I'd heard they were working on their *Jazz* documentary miniseries. My friend Curt Flood had worked with them on their *Baseball* documentary series and gave me a contact. They replied to my inquiry politely and said they'd get back to me, but they never did. I always suspected Stalebread and the Razzy Dazzy Spasm Band would not have fit comfortably into their jazz history narrative.

For the past 25 years of my artistic life, I have been mostly at my easel working in oils on canvas, along with freelancing as a cartoonist to support myself as a painter. In 2000 I self-published my first book of short stories, *MOJOS volume one*.

In 2014, I contacted one of Stalebread's granddaughters and told her of my plan to write this book. She was reluctant to talk with me at first, but finally agreed. I asked for permission to research their private family tree on Ancestry.com. She politely informed me that she and another relative had made the family account private because they intended to write their own book about their grandfather. Out of respect for the Lacoume family, I offered them my entire collection of research material to use for their book. My offer was ignored, so once again, I was on my own. I waited a full year to give them a head start before I began writing this book in earnest.

After moving with my family from New Orleans to Colorado in the mid-1990s, Rose and I continued to chat on the phone once in a while. We had been exchanging Christmas cards for years, and I was worried when I did not receive her card in 2004. The following year, New Orleans was hit by Hurricane Katrina. I could not reach Rose or Peter by phone, and I was even more worried by December of 2005 when again no Christmas card arrived. The Weavers lived not far from the breach in the levee caused by Hurricane Katrina. It was a few years ago that I learned from one of her nieces that Rose had died in 2004, and that Peter had passed away a few months later. I took some solace in knowing Peter and Rose had passed before Katrina devastated their beloved New Orleans. I hope this book preserves her father's legacy and would please them both.

—*Michael Shurtz, Boulder, Colorado, 2025*

PRELUDE: THE SPANISH TINGE

Of course, you have to have these little tinges of Spanish in it,
in order to play real good jazz.
—Ferdinand "Jelly Roll" Morton

Captain Payén's Eighth Cavalry Mexican Band, Payén seated at right

The musical innovation known as the Spanish tinge was
introduced in New Orleans at the World's Industrial and

Cotton and Centennial Exposition in 1884 by Payén's Eighth Cavalry Mexican Band and Orchestra. Captain Encarnación Payén and his troops were goodwill ambassadors dispatched to New Orleans by the president of Mexico, Porfirio Díaz. They were stationed in New Orleans for the duration of the Exposition, which ran from December 1884 until June of 1885. One million attendees passed through the turnstiles during the Exposition's six-month existence to experience the showcase of inventions, natural resources, and trade among the Americas.

Mexico was a major financial contributor to the World's Industrial and Cotton Centennial Exposition, its government's contribution matching the $200,000 from the United States. The City of New Orleans' own investment of $200,000, on the other hand, vanished, stolen by a city administrator who fled the country.

Mexico's presence at the fairgrounds was conspicuous. The main bandstand was the center of attention at the exposition, and The Eighth Cavalry Mexican Band and Orchestra was the house band. The Mexicans' two-story Victorian barracks stood behind the bandstand. It was their home-away-from-home. Next to the bandstand stood an octagonal Victorian structure that showcased Mexico's national geology exhibit. This building, the crown jewel of the Exposition, was filled with glistening gems, ores, and precious metals.

This was the dawning of the Age of Electricity, and the Industrial Exposition was a showcase for the future. Vaunting the powerful service of electricity, the fair was illuminated by thousands of bulbs inside and out, and the massive exposition hall was air-conditioned by large electric ceiling fans. The mass production of cotton candy, ice cream, snowballs, and more was also made possible by the advent of electricity.

World's Industrial and Cotton Centennial Exposition, 1884

One other important revolutionary precursor of modern life presented at the Exposition was Captain Payén's festive and buoyant music. The Mexican bandleader unleashed a revolutionary syncopated sound on the city of New Orleans, a delightful rhythm known as *habanera.*

Payén's versatile Eighth Cavalry Mexican Band and Orchestra played waltzes, marches, mazurkas, cakewalks, and more. Popular music was in great demand all across the United States, and Captain Payén chose the latest, most familiar songs, adding his own habanera flair. American audiences largely were unacquainted with the Cuban syncopation that gave habanera its lilt, but they were instantly charmed by Payén's rhythmic innovations and arrangements. Payén's concerts at the World's Centennial Cotton and Industry Exposition are cited as the spark that ignited the American embrace of habanera. Payén's band's use of unconventional instruments such as conch shells and tin cans also intrigued the Expo's vast audiences.

The Mexican bandleader's repertoire was peppered with habanera rearrangements of standard songs. Captain Payén's son-in-law violinist and composer Juventino Rosas wrote a waltz with an infectious lilt, "Sobre Las Olas (Over the Waves)," which became the first international habanera hit. Musicians in the audience felt it, and the audiences bounced to it. Another novelty the Mexican orchestra introduced was the instrumental solo, played with unprecedented freedom and creativity. Musicians who heard this found habanera very adaptable to this innovation.

Captain Payén's most popular musician with audiences was saxophonist Florenzo Ramos, credited as the first saxophonist to perform saxophone solos. The saxophone was a relatively new instrument, having been invented in 1846.

Captain Payén put his star in front of the band, and audiences fell in love with Florenzo's showy saxophone solos.

New Orleans had many theatres and musical venues back then, all with orchestras in pits and bands on bandstands. Sure enough, under Payén's influence, local musicians began experimenting with this new tinge called "hot" music. During intermissions, it became popular with some of these pit musicians to stay seated and fool around with syncopations among themselves rather than join the others for refreshments in the hallway. Some audience members stayed in their seats during intermissions to listen to these improvisations. Just like Alexis Korner and Cyril Davies during Chris Barber's intermissions at The Marquee Club in London, audiences were being given a treat—"lagniappe," as it's called in New Orleans.

The syncopation introduced by Payén also influenced popular dance. Centuries-old ballroom dancing was becoming overshadowed by this modern phenomenon that encouraged self-expression in dance. Instead of perfectly executing steps and sequences, couples could finally express their individuality in response to the upbeat rhythms. This new style of dance was sometimes referred to as "bent knee dancing."

Mexican band member Juventino Rosas had composed a traditional waltz for Payén's band, but by adding the Spanish tinge, "Sobre Las Olas" paved the way for modern music and modern dance. Popular music in New Orleans was getting hot, thanks to Captain Payén.

The Eighth Cavalry Mexican Band was so popular during their six-month-stay in New Orleans that smaller ensembles of musicians from their ranks were invited to play music all over New Orleans, at picnics, parties, benefit concerts, and other functions. The Mexican musicians were being invited to sit in with New Orleans bands, and were treated as guests of honor. This enthusiastic welcome encouraged a number of Payén's orchestra members to reside in New Orleans permanently after their company's contracted engagement came to an end.

Payén's expatriates settled into the diverse northeast corner of the French Quarter, with its many Spaniards, Mexicans, and Puerto Ricans. They supported themselves and their families by working as professional musicians, playing in New Orleans bands and pit orchestras, and as private music tutors who educated rising musicians. The Mexican talent pool included another saxophonist named Vascarro, who would become the uncle of jazz musician Alcide "Yellow" Nunez, and the distinguished music teachers Louis Chaligny and Wallace Cutchey, who taught Bunk Johnson.[1] Mexican trombonist Manuel Guerra found plenty of work as a musician and teacher, and mentored future jazz great Eddie Edwards[2].

The most prominent of these Mexican expatriate musicians was Florenzo Ramos. After settling in New Orleans, Florenzo published a popular song titled "Dorados Ensueños." The multitalented Ramos made his living teaching music and playing saxophone, for a time joining "Papa Jack" Laine's Reliance Brass Band. Florenzo was also a founding member of the Musicians Union, New

1. Willie Gary "Bunk" Johnson (1879–1949) was a prominent jazz trumpeter in New Orleans.
2. Edwin Branford "Eddie" Edwards (1891–1963) was an early jazz trombonist who was a member of the Original Dixieland Jass Band.

Orleans' Local 174. For a stint in the early 1920s, the elderly saxophonist Florenzo played with the Fischbein-Williams Syncopators at the LaVida Dance Hall, where a middle-aged Stalebread, the orchestra's banjo player, sat next to him.

The renowned Latin musicians in Captain Payén's Eighth Cavalry Band at the birth of jazz continued to contribute to the growing hot music scene in New Orleans.

PART ONE
OVER THE WAVES

1. A Natural-Born Musician

Every bird must sing with its own throat.
—Henrik Ibsen

Emile August Lacoume II was born in New Orleans on September 22, 1885. He was the first-born child of Emile August Lacoume, a French immigrant of aristocratic lineage, and Jennie Strain, of German and Italian descent. The Lacoumes lived in the French Quarter. In their neighborhood mix of commercial and residential occupants, the Lacoumes' apartment was on the ground floor, where their front stoop met the flagstone pavement of Exchange Alley.

Emile and Jennie waited two years after their son Emile's birth to get married. On Tuesday, June 28, 1887, they tied the knot in St. Louis Cathedral, just down the street from their apartment. Their second child, Emma Aloysius, was born about a year after they married.

The Lacoumes' French Quarter neighborhood, Exchange Alley

The elder Emile was proud of his French lineage, and was fond of telling young Emile about their aristocratic ancestors, who included the Dukes of Bordeaux. Two pieces of heirloom furniture adorned their simple living room, brought from France to New Orleans in 1846 by young Emile's grandfather, Charles Lacoume. The chair and matching ottoman were upholstered in chartreuse chenille with a gold *fleur-de-lis* motif. These prized possessions were off-limits to the children unless they sat on their mother's or father's lap. The children had their own favorite spots in their cozy apartment. Emma liked to perch on top of the couch and watch the activity in Exchange Alley. She liked to put her dolls on the windowsill, posing a doll to wave to the passersby. The Lacoumes' third child, christened James Nolan Lacoume, was born in 1891.

Young Emile's favorite spot was at the kitchen table, where he tinkered with items he had scavenged in the neighborhood. He treasured the harmonica he found around the corner in front of the Merchants' Exchange. He revived the petrified harmonica by taking it apart and cleaning each reed, carefully swabbing the holes and giving all of the metal parts a thin coat of his mother's sewing machine oil.

Emile mastered the instrument by imitating his mother while she played her English concertina and sang. She often encouraged him with a quote from her favorite playwright, Ibsen: "Each bird must sing with its own throat." Jennie repeated each song until he could play it back to her. She performed in both French and English, and with a wealth of material to choose from, mother and son sang together every day. "Froggy Went a Courtin'" was the first full song he learned to sing.

When Emile's father arrived home from work, he would join them singing Creole folk songs, like "Maison Denise" and "Remon." Jennie also knew scores of English and Irish folk songs that her immigrant parents had brought over from England. Young Emile was fascinated by tales of murder in songs like "Matty Groves" and "Little Sadie." His favorite ballads were the ones about highwaymen like Patrick Fleming from "Whiskey in the Jar," and rogues like Johnny Faa and Black Jack Davey, who he had heard about in "Raggle Taggle Gypsy" and "Roving Gambler." The mother-son duo also learned many popular songs of the day, including "Botany Bay," "Johnny Get Your Gun," and one of Emile's favorites, "Two Lovely Black Eyes, Oh, What a Surprise."

By the time Emile was six years old, Jennie added French opera and classical music to their repertoire. The duo played Rossini's "William Tell Overture" and Offenbach's "Can Can." Little Emma loved bouncing to these tunes. Jennie and her son were also very fond of New Orleans native classical composer Louis Gottschalk's masterpieces "La Gallina," "The Banjo," and "Tournament Galop." Jennie played these melodies on her concertina and Emile learned them on his harmonica.

Jennie Strain was born to English immigrants in Toledo, Ohio, and had grown up in Iowa. A theatrical performer at an early age, she dreamed of becoming a professional opera singer. Music was her passion, and, to attain her dream, she learned to speak and read in French. At age twenty-three, Jennie was recruited by The French Opera Company of New Orleans, so she moved there from Ohio in 1880. Jennie Strain was employed by the French Opera company for five years before Emile was born.

The expectant mother had hidden her pregnancy with Emile up until two weeks before his delivery. Jennie liked to remind Emile Jr. that he had been on stage five times a week before he was even born: "That's why I call you my natural-born musician." she'd insist. According to Jennie, he also attended his first concert before he was born. His mother told him, "I was pregnant with you when Father and I went to see Payén's Eighth Cavalry Mexican Orchestra at the World's Industrial and Cotton Centennial Exposition. That was the first time I felt you moving around in there, and you haven't stopped moving to the music since!"

2. MEXICAN MANIA

All of that weird, sweet nature which characterizes the music of Mexico and has been justly popular.
— Junius Hart, *Mexican Series* sheet music

Jennie began collecting sheet music when she was a little girl, starting with her parents' dog-eared broadsides from England. Birthday presents and Christmas gifts from her parents always included a broadside leaflet, and her favorite presents were French opera portfolios.

In 1889, local music publisher and music store owner Junius Hart finally capitalized on Captain Payén's music that captivated audiences at the World's Centennial Cotton and Industry Exposition. It's curious why Hart waited four years to release his *Mexican Series*, considering Payén's popularity in New Orleans after 1885. It is especially puzzling given the infectious Spanish tinge, which had already taken hold among many local musicians. At any rate, Payén's sheet music was finally available and selling like hotcakes.

The Junius Hart Music House was located at the corner of Canal and Burgundy on the up-river side of Canal Street. The piano showroom was on the first floor and his print shop and publishing company was on the second floor. During the Exposition, Hart dispatched his piano demonstrator, William Taylor Francis, to attend each of the Eighth Cavalry Mexican Band's performances and transcribe what he heard. Francis, an accomplished composer in his own right, compiled a treasure trove of charts.

When Hart published these charts as his *Mexican Series*, the cover bore portraits of Francis and Hart, and was titled *Mexican Arrangements for Piano by W.T. Francis*. The publisher advertised the series as containing "all of that weird, sweet nature which characterizes the music of Mexico and has become justly popular." The first edition of the *Mexican Series* immediately sold out. Hart kept his printing press humming to satisfy the public's demand for this infectious music. The publisher printed a full portfolio of Francis' collection.

The following year, in 1890, Francis was working down the street as a piano demonstrator for another Canal Street music store owner and publisher, Louis Grunewald. Mr. Grunewald paid Francis for his Payén charts and Grunewald published his own edition of Payén's music, which he titled *Souvenirs of the Famous Band of the Eighth Mexican Cavalry as Played at the World's Exposition at New Orleans.* There are no records of any disputes over publishing rights between Grunewald and Hart. Francis seems to have been free to market his charts as he pleased. Following Grunewald's successful publication, the New York music publishers W.D. Wetford and A.W. Pond put out their own copycat edition, which did not credit W.T. Francis. As if trying to outdo those previous publications, Wetford & Pond's title was *Beautiful Gems: Played by the World-Renowned Mexican Military Band with Great Success at the World's Cotton Centennial Exposition, New Orleans La., and through Their United States Tour.*

These opportunistic publishers were not worried about one another, as none of the three could keep up with the public's demand for Payén material. Junius Hart had confidence in his sales, boasting on the cover of his second print run: "Over One Hundred Thousand Sold!"

"Sobre Las Olas (Over the Waves)," a waltz by Juventino Rosas, included in the original Hart/Francis *Mexican Series*, became a worldwide hit after the song was published as a single. Rosas' composition became the first international hit song of the modern era of hot music.

In 1891, Jennie, pregnant with her third child, bought her own copy of the Hart/Francis *Mexican Series* at Hart's Music House, and loved the many syncopated songs she could practice on her English concertina. Mother and son loved playing these songs together, especially "Over the Waves," Emile on harmonica and she on her concertina.

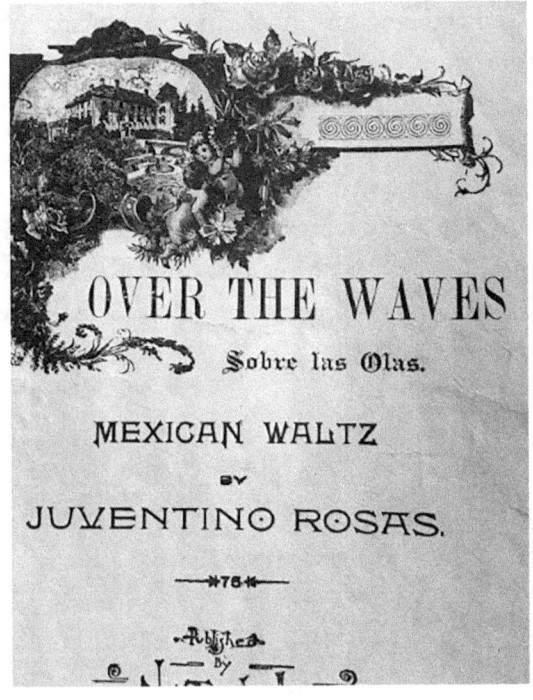

"Over the Waves" is a melody from the 1890s still popular today

On the last day of April in 1891, they were playing that song when Emile Sr. came home from work with a big surprise. He waved four tickets in front of them, saying "Payén is coming back, and we are going to see the Eighth Cavalry Mexican Band and Orchestra on the 14th! The whole family!"

Since the release of Hart's first *Mexican Series* and the subsequent editions, Captain Payén's popularity had exploded worldwide, and now he and his orchestra were returning triumphantly to New Orleans. Emile Sr. couldn't contain himself, explaining, "He's bringing sixty orchestra members this time! They're kicking off their world tour from New Orleans and making their way to Spain for the 400th year Columbus Day celebration next year."

Emile Sr. sat down in the family chair, took off his shoes, and put his feet up on the ottoman. He motioned for young Emile to sit on his lap. His father showed him the newspaper page and pointed to the article. He read the advertisement aloud:

GRUNEWALD OPERA HOUSE
60 ARTISTS
UNDER THE DIRECTION OF CAPT. E. PAYÉN.
SEATS ON SALE MONDAY.
15 CENTS, 75 CENTS AND 1 DOLLAR
GRAND CONCERT
MAY 14TH
BY THE FAMOUS MEXICAN EIGHTH CAVALRY BAND

Emile Sr. said, "Look at this. Only two weeks away. The tickets just went on sale today so I made sure I was there before the box office opened. There was already a line of people in front of me when I got there! I bet the show is sold out by now."

"Oh, Emile," Jennie swooned, "this is the best family outing we could ever ask for. Thank you!"

The printed program listed Payén's dizzying set list: "Te Amo," "Te Adoro," "America," "Brisas de Estio," "Fantasie," "Samson and Delila," "Saint-Saëns Waltz," "Jolly Friends," "Clarinet Solo," "Galop," "Kiki-Riki," "Negro Danza," and "The Telephone Mazurka," plus there would be two surprise encores.

The acoustics were brilliant in the small opera house, making the Lacoume family's 15-cent seats as good as the dollar seats. What impressed young Emile the most was Payén's use of what one reviewer the next day described as "decidedly unique instruments." Emile was enthralled with Payén's conch shells, tin cans, bells, and castanets. On their way home, the six-year-old proclaimed, "Father, I want to be in a band like Captain Payén's." Father questioned his son, "Have you given any thought to which instrument you will play? There are so many to choose from."

"I like the stringed instruments, guitars, and banjos mostly," Emile replied, "but I also like Captain Payén's tin cans and weird stuff too, especially the big seashell that sounds like a trumpet."

"Could you ever have guessed those could be instruments, Son?" his father asked him.

"Golly, no!" Emile admitted, "But now I get how almost anything can become an instrument."

A few days after the concert, Emile Sr. stopped by the pawn shop on Canal Street and put a down payment on the Creole zither he'd noticed in the window on his way to and from work. The pawnbroker brought the instrument toward his counter and tagged it before storing it in the back room. On his way home, Emile bought a paper from a newsboy who was shouting, "Read all about it! Captain Payén to stay on in New Orleans!"

Emile Sr. stopped to read the story for himself. He learned that Captain Payén had signed on for a two-week engagement at West End, the most popular amusement park on Lake Pontchartrain. Payén's Eighth Cavalry Mexican Band would be opening the season there on May 24. He rushed home to share this news.

Since attending their last concert, mother and son had been inserting the Spanish tinge into everything they played together. Emile took another trick from Payén and concocted some of his own unique instruments, employing boxes, cans, utensils, scrap metal, or anything that made interesting sounds.

This fascination became a favorite pastime. When Emile Jr. was not wandering his neighborhood scavenging, he was playing with his neighborhood friends in Exchange Alley. Indoors, at home he was often playing music with his mother, or tinkering at the kitchen table making his little instruments. Jennie knew that her boy was an "instinctive musician," and played by ear, but she also wanted him to be able to read written music. To Jennie, they were not just whiling away the hours, they were practicing. Even at his young age, her natural-born musician was becoming a practicing musician—and a dedicated one, at that.

The West End recreation park reopened with its gala

Season Inauguration on May 24, and fifteen thousand people filled the park that evening. Trains ran every ten minutes from the city to West End, and back again. The Lacoume family were among the hordes making their way to the reopening of the lakeside amusement park. This was their children's' first train ride, and the kids were thrilled. When the family arrived at West End, Jennie spread their picnic blankets and tablecloth under an oak tree not too far from the stage. Emile Sr. carried the large picnic basket and placed it in the center.

By dusk, anticipation for the evening concert was palpable. Stagehands shuffled around with last minute preparations for Payén's musical troops. Young Emile noticed the hour was drawing near, and climbed a tree above their picnic setting for a clearer view of the band. When the master of ceremonies finally came out, he introduced Payén's orchestra to fifteen thousand concertgoers, and the roar was exhilarating. The Mexican orchestra made their magnificent appearance mounting the stage in their crimson uniforms and plumed helmets.

The concert lasted much longer than the Grunewald's Opera House concert had two weeks earlier. After sunset, West End erupted with fireworks displays between songs.

This would not be the last time the Lacoume family had the opportunity to see the Mexican Band. The two-week engagement was so successful that Captain Payén was offered an extended contract at West End through June and July. He and his troops loved New Orleans so much that Capt. Payén cleared his calendar of all other bookings in order to stay. The Lacoume Family went together to the Fourth of July Celebration, which was actually held on the third that year. As with the spring concert, this performance lit up with a spectacular fireworks display. For the final encore: a rousing performance of "The Star-Spangled Banner" was augmented above by a bright splash of sparkling red, white, and blue.

Payén's Eighth Cavalry Mexican Band eventually departed New Orleans for Spain. After their extended stay, another troupe, La Orquesta Tipica Mexicana, came to the West End to fill the demand for more Mexican music. Emile Sr. bought two tickets for a very pregnant Jennie and young Emile, because the Orchestra Tipica Mexicana was led by none other than Juventino Rosas, whose "Sobre Las Olas (Over the Waves)" was mother and son's favorite song. Juventino Rosas was no longer playing with the Eighth Cavalry Band, and for that matter, he was no longer Captain Payén's son-in-law. Details regarding his departure are sketchy, though many noticed that Juventino appeared dejected during his final days with the band. Speculation had it that Rosas was caught cheating on his wife, the Payén's demure daughter. Rosas left Payén's troupe and went on to form his own band, La Orquesta Tipica Mexicana, or simply, The Mexican Band, as they were called in New Orleans.

Father stayed home with Emma that evening, while Jennie and Emile went to the lakefront concert. Mother and son were thrilled to hear "Sobre Las Olas" performed by the Orquesta Tipica Mexicana, led by Juventino Rosas himself.

Rosas brought with him a Mayan Indian band as his opening act. They surprised audiences with their exotic Aztec dress, and indigenous musical instruments like drums, conch shells, gourd-rattles, eerie whistles, and unusual looking and sounding trumpets. The ethereal whirring and droning their odd instruments made was unlike anything the New Orleans audiences had ever seen or heard before. They were otherworldly in contrast to the energetic Orquesta Tipica Mexicana. The Mayans performed one song that the audience knew and responded to with an ovation, the popular "La Paloma." Rosas loved the Mayan musicians and they were now part of his growing entourage. Emile was mesmerized by the Mayan Indians, whose rattles and drums created laconic beats.

"I want to be in a band like that," Emile told his mother on the way home.

"I thought you wanted to have a band like Captain Payén's," Jennie laughed.

Emile thought for a moment and answered, "I guess I should have my own band, so I can play however I like."

After seeing the big band up close, the music seemed to race through their blood at home. Jennie and Emile even played a game they called "Make It Hot."

Into this happy home, the Lacoumes' third child, James Nolan, arrived on August 20, 1891. It had been a very good summer for the family.

3. Family Lament

Winter turns to spring.

1893 BEGAN WITH AN EXCEPTIONALLY COLD WINTER. Fog from the Mississippi permeated the French Quarter each morning, keeping most of the neighborhood kids indoors until the sun burned it off. To pass the time inside, Emile tinkered at the kitchen table with scraps of discarded material and broken parts until he had built a miniature drum kit. Little Jimmy stared wide-eyed at the noisy gadgets, which looked like colorful toys. The bass drum was a hat box, the tom-tom an empty paint can, the snare drum was a sardine tin with woven key chains strung across the bottom, the cymbal was a coffee-can lid, and the drumsticks were two wooden spoons.

A pencil, a 12-inch ruler, a sharp pocketknife, and a pair of scissors were the only tools Emile needed to build Emma a dollhouse out of cardboard and rubber cement. Her brother decorated the interior walls with ads cut from old newspapers and magazines that featured appliances and artwork. Empty spice boxes served as furniture, while a Cracker Jack box made a fine chimney with a cotton ball for smoke. There were buttons for door handles, and pastry doilies for curtains and tablecloths. Emma loved her dollhouse.

Emile found a large block of balsa wood four inches square and carved it into a spinning top for his two-year-old brother. The top had four sides, like a dreidel, onto which he carefully carved an animal on each face: a dog, a cat, a bird, and a horse. He hammered a fat nail into the center of the top. Little Jimmy loved his top and he spun it on their hardwood floors every day.

The gift he made for his mother was a hand-held mirror with a copper-wire frame and a beaded handle. He worked on it whenever she went shopping or did laundry next door so his present would be a surprise.

Emile Sr. worked six days a week on the riverfront as an inspector of bonded cargo at Robert Carey & Company's sugar and molasses warehouse. While his father was at work, young Emile whittled a present for him. It was a walking cane made of a closet pole he found. To keep it a secret, he would sweep up the wood chips and put the cane under his bed each day before his father got home. Young Emile finished the cane in March and gave it to his father as soon as it was done. "I rubbed it down with Mom's butcher-block wax. That's how I got it so shiny." Father was impressed with the workmanship of the gift. "I'll walk with this every day. It's a fine cane, and it's the perfect height, just perfect."

Young Emile said, "I measured you without you even

knowing I was measuring you." His father walked with his custom cane to work every day, just as he'd promised.

Springtime arrived late after the harsh winter of 1893. In May, when the warm Caribbean winds blew in, Exchange Alley filled once again with children playing outdoors all day. Toward the end of May, Emile's father started using his cane more, for support. Jennie noticed and asked her husband how he was feeling.

He was not sure how to answer. "Not too good, but not too bad, just tired I suppose." After leaving work one day, Emile I was overtaken by a dizzy spell along North St. Peter Street. Thanks to his cane, he did not collapse, and made it to the long benches in front of the Cooper Shop. The thirty-seven-year-old man, otherwise seemingly in fine health, was puzzled by his experience. After he rested on the bench for a while, Father resumed his walk home. He kept this incident to himself.

The next day after returning home from work, just as he reached their front doorstep, he had another spell and his legs started giving out again. Jennie ushered him in, removing his hat, coat, and shoes, and helped him into the family chair, lifting his feet onto the ottoman. Jennie went to the telephone and called their family doctor. Dr. Oaker arrived twenty minutes later with his black leather satchel. The good doctor donned his stethoscope and listened to the sounds inside Emile's chest. He peered into his ears and eyes with a disc-shaped optical device. He finally took the patient's blood pressure and pronounced it "erratic. Stay off your feet and get plenty of bed rest. Call me immediately if you develop a headache, your eyes go blurry, your ears start ringing, you feel any numbness, or anything unusual for that matter—I don't care if it's the middle of the night."

Emile Sr. nodded his head, musing, "I'm only thirty-eight years old, and I suddenly feel twice my age." Dr. Oaker reassured him, "I'll come back tomorrow. And don't worry—we'll get to the bottom of the problem. In the meantime, Emile, just rest."

When Dr. Oaker left, the man of the house lay on the bed, and young Emile went to his side. Father smiled and said, "Don't worry, Docteur will figure it out, and I'll be fine." His father implored his weeping son, "Please don't cry. You'll get me crying, too, and you don't want that." He instructed his son, "Grab that bundle under the bed, would you?" Young Emile pulled out the package, which was tied with twine. "Now son, before you unwrap it, I want you to guess what it is."

The boy ran his hands over the heavy brown paper. He shook it, but it made no noise. He bounced it in his hands, guessing the weight. "Sort of heavy, like a breadboard," he gauged. "It's kind of square, but not really." He squeezed the package once more, conceding, "Father, I have no idea."

His father chuckled, "In that case, you had better just open the package."

Emile ripped off the twine and paper.

"It's a Creole zither!" his father told him. Emile inspected the instrument. "Look at all of these strings. There must be thirty or more!"

His father agreed, "You said you liked strings, and this had the most of any instrument in the pawn shop. It's just like the one Nonc Michel used to play," he said. Emile gave his father a hug and ran out of the room to show everyone his gift, laying it on the kitchen table for the others to see. Emile strummed his new zither, and a beautiful chord rang out.

"I had it tuned," Father called out from the bedroom.

Dr. Oaker returned the next day. Jennie stayed by her husband's bedside during the appointment. Emile entertained his siblings with his new zither so his parents and Dr. Oaker would not be disturbed. The doctor repeated his recommendation that his patient stay in bed and Jennie insisted she would see to that.

Dr. Oaker took a bottle of white pills from his bag. "Take one of these now. Put it under your tongue," he instructed Father, "and take another in six hours." After giving Father the prescription, Dr. Oaker took his pulse. The physician asked his patient to rise and walk around the small bedroom for two minutes. The doctor took another pulse reading and told his patient to lie back down.

"Docteur, I need a nap from all that exercise."

"Rest is the only thing I can prescribe just yet, but we'll get to the bottom of this. Remember," he reminded them both, "Call me any time of the day or night. Don't hesitate." The couple promised to comply. "I'll be back bright and early," Dr. Oaker reminded the couple as he left.

Fate preempted the good doctor's hopes, however, and thirty-eight-year-old Emile August Lacoume Sr. passed away in his sleep in the wee hours of Sunday morning, May 28, 1893.

Jennie woke up that morning, and realized her

husband had passed. Putting her ear to his lifeless breast, she laid by his side, grieving. In tears, she placed a call to Dr. Oaker, who expressed his sincere regrets and offered to call the coroner's office for her. As she wept, Dr. Oaker heard the children in the background crying, too. Dr. Oaker assured Jennie he and his wife would be over immediately. When they arrived, two-year-old Jimmy was bawling because the others were upset. The doctor's wife picked Jimmy up to console him. Five-year-old Emma was upset too, but calmed down once Jimmy did. Young Emile was speechless, sitting in his parents' bedroom at their bedside, holding his father's lifeless hand. Dr. Oaker talked with Jennie at the kitchen table, offering her a pill to calm her nerves, but Jennie declined. "Thank you, Doctor, but I'll pull myself together."

Jennie arranged for her husband's funeral services and his burial, and once these matters were taken care of, she had time to worry about her family's future. She had not worked outside the home in almost eight years. Emile Jr. understood he needed to step up and become "the man of the house." While Jennie attended to her responsibilities that week, her son assumed all her household chores, including caring for Emma and Jimmy. He thought about his neighborhood hustle of shining shoes for pennies and knew that shoeshines would not provide enough income to keep his family afloat.

Young Emile did not know much about finances, but he had often heard his parents discussing their bills. He understood that, with two little children still hanging on her apron strings, his mother had little chance of getting a job outside their home. Furthermore, Emile had learned of life's various struggles by listening to his father read newspapers aloud in the family chair every day. His parents spoke French while discussing the stories of the day in *The New Orleans Bee*, the daily French-language newspaper. Emile spoke French, too, and heard those stories. Some of the accounts detailed the French Opera's financial woes and eminent bankruptcy. Father tried to explain to his son what bankruptcy meant. Emile's parents had recently attended a benefit concert for stranded performers and other French Opera House company members, many Jennie's good friends, trying to raise money for their passage back to France. All Emile knew was that there was no employment in New Orleans at this time for French opera singers. Hearing his father grumble about the country's oncoming "economic depression," the youngster knew from his father's tone that this was bad, whatever it meant. His father had no family members near New Orleans that he knew of. For the first time in his life, Emile was forced to think about his family's future.

The French Opera House, New Orleans' premier cultural and social center

The French Opera House, interior

4. NEWSBOYS

All newsboys have nicknames

ABOUT A MONTH EARLIER, YOUNG EMILE'S SIXTEEN-year-old neighbor Jacques Dupree had said to him, "We should talk about you taking over my corner sometime. I'm getting a job with the city and I can see that you get my camp." Now Emile walked over to Jacques' place, and Jacques again offered Emile his newspaper "camp." The boys discussed the arrangement and shook hands.

After Jacques offered him the position, Emile went back home, sat his mother down at the kitchen table and declared he would be the new breadwinner of the family.

At just seven years of age, Emile told his mother, "'I want Emma and Jimmy to have the education we never had. I'm going to work Jacques' camp and sell papers!" Emile's announcement brought a smile to his mother's face.

The next morning after breakfast, the little man of the family got up from the table and donned his cap. "I'm meeting Jacques in a few minutes. Gotta go." He kissed his mother, sister, and baby brother goodbye.

Boys posing for photo outside the Newsboys' Home

From their front stoop, Emile looked down Exchange Alley to Canal Street, with its swarms of pedestrians, streetcars, carriages, delivery wagons, and bicycles. He and his neighborhood pals often went to the end of Exchange Alley and observed the hubbub. Once they witnessed the stabbing of the notorious pickpocket Cat Paws. It was a gruesome incident that neighborhood kids still talked about.

Jacques Dupree met Emile on his front stoop. "I'm glad you decided to take me up on my offer," Jacques said. "I'm starting with the city on Monday." Over the previous ten years, Jacques had made a good living as a newsboy on the French Quarter corner of Royal and Canal, and was now one of the oldest newsboys on the streets. Invariably, when newsboys became young men, they gave up the trade in favor of adult careers. Jacques had landed a job as an apprentice in the City Works Department. On this day, Jacques bequeathed his street-corner newspaper camp to Emile.

All newsboys had nicknames, and Jacques Dupree was known on the streets as Jack Dup. Jack explained to Emile that sooner or later, someone would give him a nickname, too. "That's just what we do. Mangling someone's name can start a fight and there are a lot of hard names to pronounce out here, especially those Sicilian ones. On the streets, I go by Jack Dup, but you can believe I put my real name on my City Works application: Jacques Vincent Dupree."

Emile stood up, tucked his shirttails into his waist, and said, "Let's go, Jack!"

Jack looked down at Emile's feet, saying, "You'll be wanting to leave your shoes at home—we're going out to sell newspapers." The new recruit sat back down and obeyed his first orders.

"Well," said Emile, trying to understand, "us kids all run barefoot around here in the neighborhood 'cause the pavers are smooth in the Quarter. I know Canal Street's always muddy—but what about the other streets, those American streets? I hear some of their potholes are terrible."

Jack replied, "Yep. French Quarter flagstone is easy on bare feet. Those American streets everywhere else are flat enough, which is great, but they're lousy with potholes. It's hard running those streets in the rain. You can't tell the difference between a puddle and a pothole. You get a broken ankle and you got yourself some serious trouble out there, Emile."

"I just thought everyone wore shoes on the American streets."

Jack pointed at his own bare feet and said, "I got two pairs of shoes at home, but I never wear 'em when I'm out hawking papers. All us newsboys start off poor and don't own a pair of shoes. Work hard selling papers and soon you can afford your own brand-new pair of shoes. First thing to know is, you don't want to wear them when you're running the streets. Can't stand the thought of scuffing 'em up, and that's that with that." Jack let Emile in on another newsboy maxim. "When I first became a newsboy, I was told, 'You sell more newspapers when you're barefoot.'"

"Well," ventured Emile, "if newsboys always go barefoot, how can they tell if that was true?"

"Exactamundo!" Jack smiled at his disciple's quick wit. "There wasn't anything to disprove it, so that made it a superstition. Every newsboy believes they're a little bit luckier than if they'd been wearing shoes—and now it's just who we are, and how we're expected to look."

Without further delay, Emile took off his shoes, opened his front door, and set his shoes inside.

His mother saw this and asked, "Won't you be wanting to wear your shoes, Son?"

Emile blew her a kiss goodbye. "I'll explain later, Mom."

He closed the door behind him, saying, "Okay, Jack, I'm ready to be a newsboy. Bare feet hitting the American streets!"

The waters in the gutters [of New Orleans] used to be stagnant and slimy, and a potent disease-breeder; but the gutters are flushed now, two or three times a day, by powerful machinery; in many of the gutters the water never stands still, but has a steady current. Other sanitary improvements have been made; and with such effect that New Orleans claims to be (during long intervals between the occasional yellow fever assaults) one of the health-iest cities in the Union.

— MARK TWAIN, *LIFE ON THE MISSISSIPPI*

They marched down Exchange Alley side-by-side toward Canal Street with Jack advising Emile, "Now, don't worry about your bare feet getting dirty. Just keep an eye on where you're stepping to avoid broken glass and such. That's the most important thing about running the streets barefoot." Jack gave his charge another piece of advice: "Stare at the ground in front of your feet while you walk. A sprained ankle can really cost you, a broken ankle can really cost you, but what's worse is a gash. An amputation can cost you a leg. Absolutely can't afford to get a foot cut up. Cardinal rule, buddy boy: Look down and step lightly. Infections cause most of the amputations you'll see on kids. It's a shame, but it happens. Little Louie Little got his nickname changed from Lucky to Unlucky that way. Easy to spot Unlucky with his crutch. Another kid you'll come across, Cherry Cola, he's missing half a leg, just below the knee. He got gangrene and they had to amputate—couldn't save the bottom of it. Anyway, the mud is no problem, you can rinse that off easy enough. Most of the big streets are flushed pretty often. The gutters flow with pretty clean water, for foot washing. The water department got some powerful machinery for flushing the big streets. I was hoping they'd place me in the water department, but they're placing me in the streetcar sheds uptown."

Jack and Emile got to the end of the alley and stepped out onto Canal Street, where a whirlwind of traffic made the two jaywalkers bob and weave across the one-hundred-seventy-foot expanse. Just when their feet had become incredibly dirty, sure enough, the boys found clean water flowing down the gutters on the other side.

"We need to go to Printers' Row and get you signed up. The dispatcher's office is next to their loading dock in

Natchez Alley. All of the newspaper dispatcher's offices are around back in Natchez Alley."

Printers' Row was in the downtown Central Business District and Natchez Alley was on the back of Printer's Row. Mule-drawn drayage wagons were always coming and going from the delivery docks. These were the loading docks for *The States*, *The Picayune*, and some smaller papers. The drayage wagons had duck canvas tarps strapping down their loads, to protect the fresh newspapers. Natchez Alley was continuously busy with wagons and newsboys. They heard Jack's name called out a few times as the pair walked to *The States'* loading dock and entered the dispatch office. In the office was a man sitting at his desk wearing a black bowler hat. In front of his typewriter was a nameplate that read "Mr. Mac."

Mac tipped his hat to greet the arrivals without looking up from his newspaper. Jack cleared his throat and introduced Emile, which got Mr. Mac to put down his paper and look up. Jack explained to his dispatcher that he was giving his spot to Emile. Mac handed the newbie a clipboard. "Put your name next to Jack's," he told the boy. Mac shook Jack's hand and wished him well in his new career. He shook Emile's hand, too, saying, "Welcome to *The States*, Lacoume. Grab your stack at the counter on your way out. See you tomorrow. If you need more, a wagon passes by your camp every hour. Grab a bundle. Yell to him what you took and he'll mark it in his book. Pay up here in the morning when you come in for your first stack of the day. That's how it works, Lacoume."

The torch had officially been passed. After leaving the dispatch office, Jack took Emile over to the counter to sign out his first full bundle of newspapers. There was a short stack of yesterday's papers on the floor, which were free, and Jack handed a couple of those to Emile.

"I always take along two of yesterday's papers when I pick up today's first stack." Jack smudged his thumb over the day-old and said, "See, the ink is dry." He showed Emile his clean thumb. "You put one on the bottom and one on top and sandwich your stack. One keeps the fresh ink off my sleeves, and the other keeps it off my shoulders. Then, when I get to my camp, I drop the day-old paper on the sidewalk and place the fresh stack on top of it, and take the other day-old paper and put that on top of the stack. Now, not everyone does the top one like me. Some newsboys are superstitious about burying today's headlines under yesterday's, which I understand, but I don't care. They say it's bad luck, but I do it because I can sit on my stack if I need to, and also, I like standing on my stack sometimes, so I just forget about that particular superstition and take my chances. Gotta pick your superstitions. There's too many to take 'em all on, right? Besides, I'm waving today's paper in front of everyone's faces and shouting today's headlines. That's good enough."

The novice followed Jack's instructions, hoisting his stack onto his shoulder. Some of the newsboys noticed Jack didn't have a stack when he was leaving the newspaper offices, and one of them ambled up, saying, "So, the rumor is true!" and Jack nodded.

"Yep, Izzie. I'm through selling ink."

"Take care, Jack Dup!" another boy hollered from across the alleyway.

From Natchez Alley, Jack and Emile went directly to

his corner of Canal and Royal. When they arrived, Jack put his arm around the lamppost and hugged it. "I'm going to miss this spot," he said wistfully, "I've had this camp since I was your age. It's been good to me. It will be good to you too, little buddy."

Emile's schooling continued. "You'll want to come up with a good shout," Jack told his successor. "Get something to grab people's attention, because everything moves real fast on Canal Street. When I was your size, I used to stand on my stack just to be seen. Your shout goes further from the top of your stack, too. Get a good shout, and you'll get your repeat customers, and your repeats will become your regulars, see? I call my regulars my 'Steadies.' That's why my shout has always been, 'Hey Steadies, ready for my Steadies.' You can switch it up with your 'Read all about it!' shouts, too. Just make them want to buy from you."

Jack Dup finished his street-corner tutorial, confident that his protege would do fine. The initiate was nervous at first, but when Jack Dup left him on his own, Emile relaxed and launched into the standard newsboy shout, "Extra! Extra! Read all about it!" Only he didn't see a particularly compelling headline on the front page, so he pulled out his harmonica and played "Maison Denise," "Raggle Taggle Gypsy," and "La Banjo."

Two businessmen stopped for their morning editions and stayed a couple minutes for the music. Emile sold out his first stack and got a second one from the delivery wagon when it came by at 9:20. At 11:40, the same delivery wagon came by again. This time it took Emile's leftover Morning Editions and left him with two stacks of afternoon editions. The bundles were still warm—"hot off the press," as the saying goes. His first day went very well.

When he got back home in the afternoon, Emma and Jimmy met their brother at the door. Jennie was at the kitchen table when Emile emptied his pockets, which were loaded with coins. His family marveled at the pile. "I get to keep half of this," the proud breadwinner told them.

"Did you meet any other newsboys?" his mother asked.

"I saw a lot of them in Natchez Alley when I got signed up, but I didn't really meet any. They all know Jacques though. They call him Jack Dup, and they all look up to him."

"Jacques is a fine young man," his mother said. "I bet they'll give you a nickname, too."

Jennie placed a napkin and spoon next to his bowl of gumbo. He dug right in, and hardly had the air to say, "No doubt. I'm awful hungry—couldn't leave my camp all day!"

The following day, Emile retraced his route back to Natchez Alley, about a five-minute walk from home. When he got to *The States'* loading dock, he went into the office and paid Mr. Mac for yesterday's papers. He went out to the counter and signed for a large stack.

"Don't forget a couple of yesterday's papers," the kid in line behind him suggested.

"Thanks, almost forgot," confessed the newbie. With stacks on their shoulders, they both walked outside.

"You're Jack Dup's replacement, I heard." the newsboy said to Emile.

"Yep. Jack's my neighbor. He just got a job with the city."

"I heard about that too. You're lucky to get Jack's camp. It's one of the best corners in the whole city. You'll do well there," he promised.

"Thanks. I'm Emile, by the way."

"They call me Warm Gravy. Say Emile, you should stop by the Newsboys' Home sometime. That's where I live, right over there." Warm Gravy pointed to a wooden building just across the alleyway, at four stories the tallest building in Natchez Alley. The Newsboys' Home was an orphanage run by nuns and home to newsboys and potential newsboys. The boys ranged from infants to teenagers.

"We're getting a gymnasium with a basketball court," Warm Gravy informed him.

"Never have played, but I'd really like to learn," answered Emile. He'd made his first friend at his new job and Warm Gravy would introduce him to other boys from the orphanage. Days turned to weeks, weeks into months, and customers grew into a large number of "steadies." As months passed, the family bank account grew, and before the year was out, Emile was matching his father's income, bringing the family out of financial danger. Beyond this, his goal was to earn enough money to pay tuition for Emma and Jimmy when they came of school age as he had promised his mother from the start.

Emile eventually took Warm Gravy up on his invitation. After the gym was completed, Emile started hanging out with the orphans at their Newsboys' Home daily. Of the many orphans, four were Warm Gravy's good pals. They played pick-up basketball games, and the basketball shooting game known as "Horse." Warm Gravy's friends were Chinee and the brothers Cajun and Monk. Another newsboy who became their friend was Family Haircut. Like Emile, Family Haircut was not an orphan. He lived with his family above his grandfather's barbershop.

As Jack Dup had instructed him to, Emile came up with a shout: "Hidee hidee hidee hi!" He encouraged his customers to respond in kind, "Hidee hidee hidee hi!" He'd follow this with, "Hodee hodee hodee ho!" and coaxed a second response, "Hodee hodee hodee ho!" Decades later, Cab Calloway wrote a song called "The Hi De Ho Man" and included this same call-and-response chant in his signature song "Minnie the Moocher." It is unclear where or when that chant originated; it could have been a stevedore's sea shanty or a field holler, for all we know.

Emile came up with another shout: "*Hot* cha cha cha cha!" He loved lingering on the word *hot*. "*Hot* cha cha cha cha!" It became his go-to response to sales, tips, and anything he felt like emphasizing. (In Chapter Seventeen, I share how Jimmy Durante came to adopt this as his own signature catchphrase.)

5. ORPHANS AND HALF-ORPHANS

Pretty soon I had 'em like a well-oiled machine!
—Stalebread

THE 1890S MARKED THE ERA OF YELLOW JOURNALISM, in which newspaper publishers had perfected the art of inventing hyperbolic headlines to sell more papers. "If it bleeds, it leads," was the motto of these competitive publishers. Newsboys shouted the headlines with great urgency. This was their primary gimmick, along with their own personal shouts. Headlines were the juicy bait.

During the economic depression, known as the Panic of 1893, the newspapers were also covering a variety of forms of strife, from violent labor strikes to political crusades, to high unemployment rates. To generate content, publishers often embedded reporters in situations like Coxey's Army, the ragtag grassroots surge of unemployed workers who protesting their plight in massive cross-country treks toward the nation's capital in 1894. During troubling times like these, the entire country marched to the hysterical drumbeat of the press. Newspapers even went so far as to incite wars to generate sensational headlines and coverage, as was the case in the lead-up to the Spanish-American War. There was no shortage of incendiary headlines in the 1890s.

Intuitively, Emile chose to dish up levity to his customers, while at the same time serving as the bearer of bad news. While most newsboys shouted "Extra! Extra!" with extra dread, Emile used extra humor. His scat singing, dancing, and goofy antics, known as "hokum," took the edge off the grim news. His salesmanship made him the most successful newsboy in the city.

When in line for their stacks at the dispatcher's office, Emile was often congratulated by his friends. Likewise, he was proud to be considered part of their brotherhood.

The Society of Saint Vincent de Paul, with the Sisters of Mercy of St. Adolphus, opened the Newsboys' Home in 1879, before moving the orphanage and boys' shelter to the four-story building across Natchez Alley from *The States*, *The Picayune*, and the other newspapers on Printer's Row.

The boys received the motherly love of the nuns, as well as the fatherly influence of a couple of good male role models. Father Nicholas was the priest who served them the sacraments in the Home's chapel, and more than that, he was the patriarch of the Newsboys' orphanage. Father Nicholas was not an authoritarian; he kept them in line with kindness. The little carpenter next door, Chris Nielsen, was another solid male role model for the boys; fixing what was broken and building what was needed for their home. Chris had recently built the gymnasium on the first floor, and in doing so, became a saint in their eyes. Mr. Nielsen built a fine indoor half-court.

Emile often spoke of his deceased father to his friends. All the boys had heard about his family lineage, and how he came from French aristocracy, the dukes of Burgundy. So his newsboy friends nicknamed him "Duke," or "The Duke."

Duke's routine was to bring home his daily earnings to his mother and run back to Natchez Alley, where he would join his friends and stay for supper at the Newsboys' Home. For supper, Old Mother Kelly served stew and beans and bread for ten cents. Duke also began attending night school with his pals on the second floor of the Home.

He spent so much of his free time at the Newsboys' Home that he was considered what the orphans called a "half-orphan." He was not in need of a family or a home but he enjoyed the camaraderie at the newsboys' orphanage. Some of the half-orphans were homeless and on a waiting list, so they would stay nearby until a bed at the Home became available for them. Other boys were avoiding abusive situations—for some, two parents at home were worse than one—and the Newsboys' Home became a refuge for those unfortunates as well. The two so-called half-orphans who had no such woes were Duke and Family Haircut.

The cardinal rule at the Home was no smoking indoors. The Home was a four-story wooden structure with two dormitory levels on top. One shuddered to think what would happen if a fire broke out.

One afternoon while lollygagging in the gym, a few of

the boys started talking about music. Some of them had been looking over Warm Gravy's shoulder at *The American Boy's Handy Book* by Daniel C. Beard, as Warm Gravy studied the chapter on building musical instruments. On the left-hand page were detailed illustrations showing how to fashion a cornstalk fiddle, and the facing page showed how to make a pumpkin-vine flute and a cane fife.

"We should make some instruments and start a band," Warm Gravy proposed, "The Duke can be our bandleader! He's got all the songs and all the moves."

The two brothers, Cajun and Monk Busey, liked the idea, as did Chinee and Family Haircut. The Duke listened intently, imagining this would-be band. It was everyone's foregone conclusion that The Duke should be their bandleader, and Warm Gravy convinced him, insisting, "You know, Duke, as our leader, it'll be your duty to name the band, pick the songs, and call all the shots. Right, boys?"

They unanimously answered with a "Hurrah!"

"Well, we will need some real instruments, fellas," was his first official proclamation, "at least a couple of factory-made instruments like my harmonica. Come to think of it, Family Haircut has his paper and comb—those two are factory-made, right?" They all laughed. "I guess we've already got enough of those factory-mades. The rest we'll just need to build. But we won't be using no corn stalks or no pumpkin vines. What we make better be good if we want to make good music."

After The Duke threw down the gauntlet, the boys shouted another "Hurrah!" to seal the deal. "One other thing," he added, "we'll play everything hot! Nothin' but hot, boys, nothin' but hot."

"Okay, then, fellas," Emile declared, "I'll get to work on figuring out our name."

The band members searched high and low for materials inspired from the *American Boy's Handy Book* to construct their own instruments. Family Haircut had his comb, which he played as an instrument when he folded a piece of silk paper over it and blew through his lips so it reverberated, sounding like a kazoo. Amazingly, he could hit notes on the paper and comb instrument—though it made his lips tingle something terrible. He also used a shiny new section of stovepipe to amplify his humble device. Warm Gravy found bottle caps and a cracker-tin lid to make a tambourine. Monk and Cajun took days scavenging for parts, hoping something could be made from the lot.

What they really needed to complete their string section was a standup bass, but they knew that a factory bass fiddle would cost much more than they could afford. The boys approached Chris Nielsen to help them build one, and they came to him with a wooden keg that Chinee found. Mr. Nielsen already had a spare table and chair leg in his shop.

All the boys crowded around Chris in his workshop while he showed them how he would construct the small bass fiddle. Chinee's instrument would be formidable.

Chris also helped the brothers Cajun and Monk with their two stringed instruments.

The workshop had an abundance of scrap material laying around. Assortments of wood, metal, glass, wire, and string were stacked on the shelves lining the walls. Mason jars of nails, bolts, and screws sat on the shelf above his workbench. Mr. Nielsen held the table leg above the keg and the chair leg beneath it. "It'll go together like this. See?"

Chris began construction right away. First, he sawed the table leg lengthwise down the middle, creating a flat neck on the front with a rounded backside—easy for holding in a small hand. The bridge was an old worn-down blackboard eraser holding the strings perfectly in place on the face of the instrument. The chair leg formed the endpin used to raise the bass off the floor, and allowing the instrument to be dramatically twirled around. This pivot-point supported any weight put upon it—with the idea, as Mr. Nielsen pointed out, that a band member could even jump onboard. The endpin ran like a beam through the body to the neck, and the carpenter set it with wood screws and glue on the inside. The strings were rubber-coated electric wires running from the top of the neck to the bottom of the body. He cut out two f' holes on each side of the bridge with his new electric router. After Mr. Nielsen finished making it, he presented it to the band. Their response was, "Bully!"

Once all of their instruments were good to go, Duke began rehearsing his boys out in Natchez Alley. A piece Duke knew they would enjoy playing was "Georgia Camp Meeting." Emile also got them to whistle songs in unison, like "Rosie O'Grady" or "The Daring Young Man on the Flying Trapeze" and, after constant drilling, and before long, The Duke began describing the outfit as "a well-oiled machine."

He said, "When we do slinky slides, let's break it up with those hesitations and then get into the bang-bang stuff!"

The Duke taught them all the physical tricks he knew from his corner antics, and made up a few new ones too, now that they were performing as a unit. They did not choreograph routines; they just learned to keep from knocking each other over.

Tired of constantly being asked when they would get their name, Duke finally came up with one and couldn't wait to tell them. Everybody knew how important it was to have a good name.

"Pick us a snazzy one," Monk insisted, with others agreeing, "Yeah, a *real* snazzy one," they all chimed in.

It had been only a week since they formed their band when their leader finally laid it on them. "Okay boys, you asked for a snazzy name and I got just what you want. Names don't get snazzier than the one I got us. We are now: The Razzy Dazzy Band!"

They all had broad grins of approval, when he spelled it out for them. "That's R-A-Z-Z-Y D-A-Z-Z-Y, double-double Zs!"

They all could not have been happier, and voiced their approval simultaneously proclaiming it, "Bully!"

Cajun said, "Gee whiz, you're right on the money with that one, Duke—a band name don't get no snazzier than Razzy Dazzy!" Each boy repeated the band's name out loud, trying it on for size. Warm Gravy proclaimed, "That's the best damn name in the entire damn history of band names!"

6. STALEBREAD

Our first performance as a band was on Royal Street between Canal and Iberville. When we began cutting loose, people didn't know what they were hearing, but they'd like it! Within five minutes that street was blocked! We passed the hat around and it got filled with coins. This crowd knew then and there that Stalebread's band was on the job.
—Stalebread

AS THE PRACTICE SESSIONS PROGRESSED, THE RAZZY Dazzy Band were finding their groove, which led to wondering when and where they would be unleashed. The Duke teased them about their debut until it became *the* topic of conversation. Each of them speculated on the possibilities. None of them saw it coming the morning the Duke showed up at the Newsboys' Home at 6:15. He ran up the stairs to the top floor, the older boys' dormitory, and he went around shaking the shoulders of his crew, announcing their imminent departure. Cajun, Monk, Warm Gravy, and Chinee got up, got dressed, and made their beds, while still half asleep. Their first order of business was to go down one floor to the younger boys' dorm and wake up their substitutes to recruit them for the day. They then descended to the dining room, where Ma Kelly was putting out the oatmeal and coffee for breakfast. Having already been summoned over the telephone, Family Haircut showed up. The six bandmembers sat at the big table to eat.

The Duke announced, "I woke up, and it just came to me. We're going downriver this morning. We can hop a train and return in the afternoon. The train to Bohemia stops in Poydras. We get off in Poydras, hit the street, make some coin, have some lunch, and come back on that same train two hours later. We debut in Poydras, boys."

Their leader explained the gig further, promising they would return "triumphant" from their sojourn with "bragging rights" and notoriety from their out-of-town debut. The Razzy Dazzy Band grabbed their instruments, walked out the back door of the Home and through Natchez Alley, and headed to the riverfront railyards. The closer they got, the more excited they grew.

"We're looking for the 603," their leader informed them. They scoured the train yard and watched as the final boxcar was coupled to Engine 603. The boys climbed into the one empty boxcar at the end of the train, and waited patiently as the 603 rolled out of the yard. The train was on its way to Bohemia, right on schedule.

The train chugged out of the yard parallel to St. Peter Street, heading downriver. It passed through the neighborhoods on the southern edge of New Orleans and slowly picked up speed. The boys sat at the edge of the boxcar, its doors slid wide open, their legs dangling out the sides. Twenty miles an hour was faster than any of them had ever moved.

Then, just as gradually as it had picked up speed, the train began decelerating. The boys looked at each other in bewilderment, and no one was more puzzled than the Duke when it became clear they were being waylaid. The train crawled into the Elysian Fields yard and came to a stop, where it was relieved of the last four boxcars, one being theirs. Hearts sank as they realized their barnstorming trip was ending before it had hardly begun. As the dejected band members sat in their boxcar, they started talking about food out of boredom as much as hunger. Soon they were searching their pockets for any sort of morsel to munch on, but all the boys produced were sticks of gum and cigarettes.

"Let's count our money," suggested Duke.

"What money?" his bandmates replied, having just turned their pockets inside out. On a normal day, they wouldn't have run off half-asleep the way they had that day. They had only a nickel among the six of them. Ever the optimist, Duke took the nickel and insisted, "Well, then, this nickel will just have to do." He promised to return with lunch for all. Even his faithful friends had a hard time believing he could pull off this feat, but they wished him luck, and started shooting dice on the boxcar floor while awaiting his return.

The Duke got his bearings and walked toward the Elysian Fields neighborhood. Near Claiborne Avenue, he found a bakery open for business. In the window he saw a hand-lettered sign: "DAY OLD BREAD: 2 LOAVES FOR 1 NICKEL."

The bandleader went in and purchased two loaves of the day-old bread.

Back at the boxcar, the boys' spirits soared when they saw Duke marching toward them, a loaf of bread under each arm. There are not many ways to get six meals out of one nickel, but their intrepid leader had found one.

"Hurrah!" all of them cheered when Duke handed up the loaves and they hoisted their triumphant leader back onboard. They passed the loaves around and Warm Gravy toasted, "To Stalebread!"

"To Stalebread!" they all toasted, waving wads of bread. His bandmates were at once saluting both their food, and their leader. From that moment on, they no longer called him Duke. His name was Stalebread.

The next day, The Razzy Dazzy Band was still chomping at the bit to make their formal debut on the streets of New Orleans as Stalebread had promised. The band wanted to brush off their misfired debut as soon as possible.

Stalebread later recalled to a journalist, "Our first performance as a band was on Royal Street between Canal and Iberville. When we began cutting loose, people didn't know what they were hearing, but they'd like it! Within five minutes that street was blocked! We passed the hat around and it got filled with coins. This crowd knew then and there that Stalebread's band was on the job."

7. The Razzy Dazzy Band

Whang-bam! We'd let 'em have it!
—Emile "Stalebread" Lacoume

AFTER THEIR SUCCESSFUL MUSICAL PREMIERE ON Royal Street, the band knew they were on to something good. It was hard for them to concentrate on their studies, but they still attended night school every weekday evening for two hours. Their classroom was on the second floor of the Newsboys' Home. Boys of all ages were taught the "'Three Rs" (reading, writing, and arithmetic—or more colloquially, "readin', writin', and 'rithmetic") and catechism. Classes began after supper and ended at nine o'clock. The nuns welcomed the so-called half-orphans to these classes, and Stalebread and Family Haircut attended regularly. The orphans in the band who lived at the Home —Warm Gravy, Chinee, Cajun, and Monk—were all naturally regulars as well.

Royal Street between Canal and Iberville

The classroom had an eight-by-five-foot blackboard mounted on the wall behind the teacher's desk. Above it hung a gothic crucifix. A globe of the world rested on a pedestal. Over the door was a white-faced clock with two black hands. Student desks occupied the rest of the room. Being newsboys who hawked the printed word, they were avid readers and good students. Just the same, when the clock hit nine, the bandmembers grabbed their instruments, ran down the stairs, hit the streets, and were ready to perform.

Sometimes they would start out playing at the foot of Canal and work their way up. Typically, they walked a couple blocks at a time, only stopping to play when it looked profitable. They'd eventually arrive at the New Orleans Passenger Station on Canal between Rampart and Basin Street. The train depot was the official face of the District, the train line bounding the city proper and the notorious eight block "red light" district, later known as Storyville. The depot's tin-covered train sheds next to the depot made a good venue for The Razzy Dazzy Band not only for sheltering them from rain, but also because the tin roofs amplified their music.

The train sheds protected and amplified The Razzy Dazzy Spasm Band

FRESH OFF THE TRAIN, YOUNG SPORTS STOOD AROUND stretching their legs and getting their bearings as others waited to board departing trains. Most nights, The Razzy Dazzy Band finished their roving around eleven o'clock. Often the boys lost track of time, and stayed out later. By midnight they usually left the depot, no longer roving but heading home to bed, exhausted at the end of their long day.

Father Nicholas' rule was that the back door facing Natchez Alley "always stayed closed, but always stayed unlocked." He did not impose curfews. Father Nicholas' rectory was next to the back door. He was the male guardian of the Newsboys' Home, as well as the spiritual shepherd to his flock. The nuns' convent was at the front of the Home, where the front doors were always locked at night. The boys' dormitories were unsupervised. The boys themselves maintained only one rule: peace and quiet. The newspaper presses hummed their industrial rhythms in Natchez Alley throughout the night, but the boys in their third- and fourth-story dormitories could still hear the music drifting from Perdido Street.

The newsboys' daily routines revolved around distributing the newspaper's morning, noon, late afternoon, and evening editions. Each of the boys in the band had younger substitutes filling in for his shifts, so the band could play on Canal's street corners during evening rush hour while their subs sold the papers back at their various camps.

The young street musicians' sole competitors were the German "Oompa" bands huffing and puffing on the busy streetcorners. The boys found them hilarious, and ribbed them for the way they dressed and kept a regimented formation. The Razzy Dazzy Band wasn't as loud as the

German bands, but what the newsboys lacked in volume, they made up for in audacity. Stalebread set up his band near any German band they came across. This rankled the Germans, who thought the barefoot boys more than just a nuisance; they were cutting into their profits. Whenever the Germans tried to shoo them away, the newsboys hurled anti-German immigrant insults from across the street. The German musicians tried to ignore them but couldn't. Often the Germans lobbed English insults back at them. When these were not enough to vent their frustration, they resorted to a tirade of shouts in their native tongue. The boys laughed at them all the more, which only further infuriated the Germans. Stalebread called these "hot battles." As Stalebread told an interviewer, "Whang-bam! We'd let 'em have it!" The gang would make such a racket that the Germans' small audiences would get distracted and look across the street to see what was happening.

The German bands naively expected the police to put an end to the turf war, so they always summoned the nearest beat officer. The Razzy Dazzy Band always vanished before the cops arrived. The beat police did not appreciate being caught between these two warring factions. Even if they could catch them, the cops couldn't charge the boys with anything, as no crime was being committed. Yet the Germans insisted a crime was taking place, and harangued the beat police for not chasing after the boys. Criminals or not, The Razzy Dazzy Band earned the beat cops' retribution for instigating this turf war.

8. The Tour

Come back anytime you want!
—Colonel Boudreaux

To defuse The Razzy Dazzy Band's conflict with the beat cops, Stalebread had an idea: he decided his band would get out of town for a few days. One of his steadies had that morning told him about an Elks Club fundraiser, a vaudeville show in Jackson, Mississippi, that still needed a band to fill the bill on Saturday night. Stalebread called the telephone number and spoke to the talent agent, Colonel Boudreaux.

The Colonel was impressed to hear that The Razzy Dazzy Band was from New Orleans, and even more so that they played nothing but hot music. "I didn't know there was a band that played nothing but hot music, but it figures if there was one, it would come out of New Orleans." The Colonel offered Stalebread top billing and six dollars. "Your name will look great up on the Elks

Lodge marquee. I'll have it up today. We'll make sure to mention you're from New Orleans, too. That will excite the folks in Jackson."

The bandleader agreed to the amount of six dollars for their set. It was not much money to travel so far for, but this was not about the money.

Stalebread picked Shreveport for their first destination, as it was as far west as you could go in Louisiana. Shreveport, he enthusiastically claimed, was "Way Out West. I bet they got real cowboys and Indians out there!" Stalebread explained to them that Jackson, Mississippi, was about 200 miles due east of Shreveport. "We'll be crossing the whole state, from one side to the other, in the comfort of a coach, not some windy boxcar. But this means we'll have to make enough coin in Shreveport to pay for our coach fares."

On Wednesday, the Newsboys' Home was buzzing with word of the "tour." The band recruited their younger substitutes to fill in at their newspaper camps while they were away. The Newsboys' Home's rules required orphans to pin a note on their pillow to secure their cots, and they also had to inform their Sister Superior, Sister Mary Rita.

Early Thursday morning, Old Mother Kelly was in her kitchen wrapping bacon and cornbread in silk paper for the six travelers. Family Haircut and Stalebread arrived and they all had oatmeal and coffee for breakfast. The city was already humming when the crew left the alley and walked down to the railyard. About two hours later their train left the yard, and finally their tour was underway.

The 300-mile train ride to Shreveport got them there

with enough time to busk, and get dinner at a seafood place. That night, a blacksmith let them sleep on a big pile of hay in his barn. The boys woke up well rested and hit the streets once again. The first few streetcorner performances got them more puzzled looks than coins.

In the late afternoon, their luck changed when they came upon a warehouse at the north end of town where an outdoor public auction was taking place. When the auction was closing down, a few dozen people still milled around. The auctioneer finished his closing patter, put down his gavel, and went inside. Before the crowd could disperse, The Razzy Dazzy Band took over the auctioneer's platform and started playing "Rosie O'Grady." The audience stayed put and more people arrived on the scene. The band had a sizeable crowd, so they passed the hat for the first time. They passed the hat again later, and once more at the end. The Razzy Dazzy Band played their hearts out while they ran through a long list of their favorite songs, entertaining the crowd for a couple hours. By the end they were worn out, but they had collected enough money for their train tickets to Jackson, with more, to boot.

In the crowd was a group of schoolgirls their age, and some teenaged girls too. Giggling, pointing, and poking each other, the girls appeared to be assessing which band-member was the cutest. Brothers and boyfriends stood behind the girls, glaring at the band. The bandmembers had to restrain themselves from flirting with the girls. Younger children mimicked the spasm dancing they were witnessing for the first time.

After their set, the band stuck around to talk with the audience.

When all was said and done, the boys carried their instruments down the dusty road. It was a mile to the train station, the departure point for all eastbound trains. They all took turns recounting the highlights of the performance, and going on about the crowd.

"I like the girls of Shreveport!" Stalebread exclaimed.

This brought out a resounding "Hurrah!" from the others.

"Shreveport girls sure are flirts," Family Haircut added. Everyone acted out the flirtations, puckering their lips and batting their eyelashes.

Stalebread admitted, "Well, we never saw no cowboys or Indians. I guess Shreveport wasn't so far west after all."

Family Haircut concurred. "Yeah, Shreveport didn't look much like Cowboy-and-Indian country."

"Too many boats, for one thing," Cajun agreed.

Warm Gravy and Cajun played "Kick the Can" along the way, while Monk and Stalebread scoured the ground for suitable rocks for their slingshots. The latter pair would often stop to take aim at the can being kicked out in front of the troupe, occasionally hitting it and changing its trajectory. Chinee was the only one who labored, under the weight of his bass fiddle. The instrument was awkward to carry, requiring him to shift it every so often from one shoulder to the other. Family Haircut carried his comb and folded silk paper in his shirt pocket. Aware of his friends hardship, Family Haircut often spelled Chinee by carrying his bass for stretches at a time and allowing Chinee to light a cigarette. Chinee would catch up until he was walking alongside Family Haircut and could put the cigarette up to his friend's lips for a drag. They would share the cigarette this way until it was gone, and Chinee would once again shoulder his load.

The dirt road was dusty, and all that Kick the Can had covered them with dust. The station agent chuckled as they filed up to his booth to purchase their tickets to Jackson. As they walked past a long mirror, they saw what had made the agent laugh at them. Once outside, they looked like housekeepers beating rugs as they flogged the dust off one another. Back inside the station in the men's restroom, the boys took turns at the sink.

Now much more presentable, they marched themselves across the street to the brightly-lit diner, The Loose Caboose Coffee and Confections. It was the perfect place to while away the next couple hours. They admired the assorted pies, pastries and cakes under the glass domes, and looked forward to having some ice cream. Also looking good behind the counter was the waitress, a middle-aged woman in a white confectioner's smock and a candy-stripe dress, "Lorraine" stitched in red over her heart.

"These are my creations, fresh this morning," Lorraine told them. The boys, in dessert heaven, swiveled on the red leather stools at the counter.

"Coffee?" she asked. They all raised their hands. The boys at the Home affectionately referred to coffee as "mother's milk," because in truth, it had been an essential part of their diet as early as they could remember.

After two couples paid their checks and left, the boys were the only customers in the cafe. They spent the remainder of their time flirting with Lorraine, showing off their instruments and singing to their muse. When at last they had to leave, Lorraine sent them off with a white paper bag filled with pralines.

The band got back to the station just as the train to Jackson began boarding. They had a passenger car all to themselves on this starry night. Each boy stretched out on his own cushioned bench seat.

"We ridin' like kings!" Stalebread announced as the train pulled out of Shreveport. They were all very pleased at the end of the long day, and let out an exhausted, "Hurrah!"

The night train from Shreveport would arrive in Jackson at 8 a.m. It made one stop in Monroe, Louisiana, in the middle of the state, in the middle of the night, while the boys slept like babies. In the Monroe train yard, a single brakeman inspected the undercarriage of every car with his lantern. After the lengthy inspection was complete, the train was cleared to go on its way to Jackson, the boys none the wiser.

They woke up around sunrise, like they did every morning. Looking out at the passing scenery, the monotonous piney woods flicked past, which lulled them back to sleep. The train decelerated long before pulling into the Jackson train station and arrived on time, as scheduled. The steward walked through the train, announcing the stop: "Jack-*SON*!" The sleepyheads gathered their things and wobbled down the aisle. Another steward stood at the bottom of the wrought-iron steps, kindly offering each boy a guiding hand down.

The boys stood on the train platform in the warm

morning light. Stalebread walked around outside the station, getting the lay of the land. When he returned, he gathered his friends, who followed him through the quiet station and out the front entrance. The center of town was only three blocks away, so they walked along Main Street to the big park in the middle of the business district. It was a quiet Saturday morning. They were happy to find a diner across the street from the park and strolled in to get breakfast. They ate donuts and drank coffee until they were ready to burst. Before leaving the diner, each of the boys availed themselves of the restroom and groomed themselves for their evening performance. They thanked the owner when they finished, and left generous tips for the waitress.

After gorging themselves on donuts, the gluttons were ready for a nap and they went over to the shady park, across the street. As they chit-chatted and lollygagged under the trees, Warm Gravy asked, "Do you have any new tricks up your sleeve for tonight?"

"You know, I hadn't thought about that yet," Stalebread admitted, surprising the others. They knew he was always cooking up some new gimmick. The conversation drifted into other topics, but Stalebread pondered the question of a good trick for the band to pull off tonight.

On the branches above him were four squirrels. They were perfectly still when he first spotted them, but without warning they suddenly took off, chasing each other through the limbs. They looked like they were playing tag, the way they bolted each time they touched each other. It became a frenzy of ricocheting squirrels, and Stalebread laughed out loud,

"Hey, guys, look up there at those squirrels!" he said, pointing. The boys immediately became an audience and cheered the squirrels on. Chinee sat up and imitated the upright posture of a squirrel frozen in its tracks. Cajun, Monk, and Warm Gravy got into the act, too, and like the squirrels, swiveled their heads back and forth. In a flash, the squirrels resumed chasing one another. Cajun, Monk, and Warm Gravy started chasing each other, too. Every so often they would all freeze, then start chasing each other and playing tag. Family Haircut never budged from his prone position on the grass. He looked over at Stalebread, who was still lying on his back, enjoying the revelation. They were both watching the shenanigans above and now all around them. "Family," Stalebread said to him, "There's our newest shtick."

Family Haircut responded with a comical grimace, "Well," he said, "that could be a train wreck on a small stage, but I think we should give it a try tonight."

Stalebread chuckled, acknowledging Family Haircut's proposition with the rejoinder, "What could possibly go wrong?" This made both of them laugh.

When Cajun, Monk, and Warm Gravy ran out of steam from rushing around like crazed varmints, they plopped themselves down next to Family Haircut and Stalebread. Now they all were on their backs facing the bushy-tailed entertainers above them.

"Boys," Stalebread said, "tonight, onstage, at some point we gonna get 'squirrelly.'"

"I hope with all that running around, no one experiences death by musical instrument—or flying squirrel," said Warm Gravy.

Stalebread and Family Haircut looked at each other and laughed, and the others laughed too. "No, I mean it." said Warm Gravy. His sincerity made everyone laugh even harder, including Warm Gravy himself.

The Elks Lodge was easy to find, being the largest building on the block. They marveled at their name, big as could be on the marquee. The Razzy Dazzy Band indeed had top billing, and below their name appeared the pronouncement, *From New Orleans!*

The boys were content to lollygag in the city park under shade trees until the end of the quiet Saturday afternoon. That evening, the caretaker opened the front door, welcoming the boys in. He introduced himself as Bill and they each introduced themselves to him. Bill pointed out the stacks of folding chairs needing to be put in rows, and the boys offered to help. The large room was soon ready, with rows of chairs in two sections with an aisle running down the middle.

Before people started arriving for the show at 6 p.m., two women opened the concession stand, and Cajun and Monk volunteered to help them start the popcorn machine. They also carried in three five-gallon buckets of lemonade and two giant coffee percolators, just like the ones at the Newsboys' Home. The ladies arranged glasses and cups and saucers on a nearby table.

The Master of Ceremonies, "Big Hal" Hallock, arrived while the patrons were filling the hall. He introduced himself, inviting the boys to have "anything they liked" at the concession stand, compliments of the Elks.

At the start of the show, Big Hal welcomed the crowd. The vaudeville show this night was a benefit, and Big Hal invited a matronly woman wearing a big corsage to speak on the importance of the new hospital for which the event was raising money. After her plea, she further implored the audience to purchase raffle tickets for the prizes on display. Big Hal thanked her, and kicked off the evening's entertainment by introducing the opening act: "Davey and Goliath." The band had popcorn and coffee while watching the opening acts from the wings.

Two buffoons introduced as "Davey and Goliath" came out and began their slapstick routine. Goliath was seven feet tall and his ridiculous clothes were too short for him. Davey was four-and-a-half feet tall and his clothes could have fit Goliath. All their gags pivoted around their physical disparity. They pretended to have mistakenly put on each other's clothes. The tall one assumed superiority and leadership, but the short one was having none of it, mocking him while ducking nimbly in and out between the slow-moving Goliath's legs. The crowd applauded, and their final gag had Davey standing on Goliath's feet—the tall one walking him offstage that way.

The second performer was a magician named The Great Carlyle, who did an assortment of tricks with his pretty assistant, Wanda. The Rabbit-in-the-Hat, Dove-up-Sleeve, and various sleights of hand pleased the audience and the boys. For their finale, stagehands wheeled out a white coffin-shaped box on a gurney. The Great Carlyle led his assistant by the arm and she clambered into the box with great fanfare. After closing the lid, the magician brandished a logger's hand saw that he allowed the audience to see more closely as he walked near the front of the stage. The saw's lethal blade, accentuated by its oversized teeth, seemed like it could indeed saw the scantily-clad woman right in half.

Returning to the coffin-like box, the magician took his saw and placed it in the slit marking the box's middle. Very slowly he sawed until he was halfway down, then paused for dramatic effect, and wiped his brow with his handkerchief as if tiring from his work, then proceeded, despite the protests from many in the audience, to saw through the coffin to the bottom, presumably right through Wanda. The Great Carlyle put down his saw and lifted the lid to free her. When she did not immediately emerge as the audience expected, he suddenly closed the lid as if reacting to the damage he had done, which created a stir in the crowd. Looking shocked, he waved desperately for the stagehands, who rushed out, ready to wheel her offstage at his command. The crowd gasped and he paused to appreciate their reaction before opening the lid again. To everyone's relief, the beautiful assistant popped up, displaying her undivided self. Wanda waved to the audience as the stagehands whisked her away triumphantly. To thundering applause, The Great Carlyle bowed profusely as he followed them offstage.

Next, a burly strongman named Harry "Haystack" Hayes appeared onstage wearing a wrestler's singlet. In his wake, two stagehands rolled a heavy barbell to the center of the stage. Oversized cannonballs were affixed on both ends of the bar, each ball inscribed "300 lbs." Haystack Hayes stood above the barbell as if he were staring it down. He raised his arms high and waved to the audience to signal he was ready to perform his feat. Lowering himself into a squat, Haystack grabbed the barbell, feigning difficulty at first, but succeeding on his second try. The crowd cheered when Haystack lifted the barbell above his head. After this feat, he dramatically lowered the barbell to waist level, then to knee level, and dropped it with a deafening BOOM on the stage, the loud thud seeming to authenticate the numbers inscribed on the balls. After this display, Haystack clasped his hands above his head and flexed his biceps in triumph, while receiving one last round of applause as he left the stage. Following his departure, the two stagehands returned for the barbell and rolled it back where it came from.

The next act was the ventriloquist Norton, with Tommy, his freckle-faced dummy. They argued back and forth about who was the "real dummy." Their argument throughout had the doll proving his point while confounding his human straight man. They ended their routine with Tommy instructing Norton when to take a bow, and when to exit. As they took their leave, Tommy chided Norton about his poor posture and stagecraft.

Following the ventriloquist act came an animal trainer with two chimpanzees dressed in children's clothes, one as a boy and one as a girl. She skipped rope while he launched peanuts into the audience with his slingshot. The two chimps leapfrogged with their master off the stage when they were done with their schtick, and this spectacular exit got roaring applause.

After the chimp act, an old man in a black suit with a long. gray beard walked somberly to center stage. He carried a large saw in one hand and a violin bow in the other. A raven perched on his shoulder. Big Hal placed a chair on the stage. He sat and began creating haunting melodies on the toothless saw with his bow. His avian accomplice remained perfectly still throughout the old man's performance. When the eerie music came to an end, the raven launched itself off the old man's shoulder and flew into the crowd. It swooped low, just above people's heads, startling everyone in the audience. In one fell swoop, the crow snatched the rhinestone hat pin from a woman in the last row before returning to its master's shoulder. The audience was astonished and the woman was aghast. The old man scolded his naughty pet, wagging his bony finger at the thief. This was clearly part of their routine, and it broke the tension in the room when the audience laughed. The man in black motioned for the woman to come and retrieve her stolen item. She timidly approached the stage, using her husband as a human shield. The wife pushed her husband forward to reclaim her hat pin. This earned another laugh from the audience and an impish smile from the old man.

The final act before The Razzy Dazzy Band were two acrobats dressed in Robin Hood leotards and tunics. The team leapt and tumbled through hoops in a variety of ways, their big crowd-pleaser coming at the end, when the acrobats tumbled with two flaming hoops. A uniformed fire marshal and the Master of Ceremonies stood at the ready with buckets of water, adding to the sense of danger in the room.

After the two acrobats tumbled offstage, Big Hal announced a fifteen-minute intermission. He reminded the audience that this was their last opportunity to purchase raffle tickets. The door prizes were on display near the refreshment stand; the electric ice cream maker churned, the table lamp shone, and the desk fan whirled, all beckoning to the prospective ticket purchasers. On the wall above them hung the grand prize, a majestic cuckoo clock. Working the room to encourage folks to buy tickets, Big Hal reminded them that all proceeds would go to a worthy charity.

After the intermission ended, the crowd leisurely settled down. The Master of Ceremonies introduced The Razzy Dazzy Band: "Ladies and gentlemen, boys and girls, without further ado, let's make welcome The Razzy Dazzy Band!" The audience applauded.

Behind the curtain, the boys huddled in a circle. Stalebread threw down the gauntlet: "Let's give Jackson something to remember us by!"

They all shouted, "Hurrah!" and marched out onto the stage.

A murmur traveled through the audience when the boys first appeared. Big Hal called out, "May I have your attention, please! Ladies and gentlemen, boys and girls, The Razzy Dazzy Band has traveled all the way from New Orleans to put on their show for us. This is Stalebread Lacoume, the leader of the band. I thought I might ask him a couple of questions before we turn them loose." The master of ceremonies put his hand on Stalebread's shoulder.

"So, Stalebread, how did your band come by the name 'Razzy Dazzy'?"

"Well," Stalebread spoke up, "We were wanting a real snazzy name, see, and Razzy Dazzy was sure snazzy." His poetic rhyming got the crowd chuckling. "We all liked them double Zs!"

Big Hal agreed, "It's a fine name, my boy, a grrreat name, as a matter of fact. Now, let me ask you this: Is it fun being on the road?"

Stalebread beamed, "It sure is! We've covered some ground. You know, we went to Shreveport first." He looked over at his bandmates, who were grinning ear-to-ear, "Then we came all the way across Louisiana to be with y'all." The audience cheered them on. The band was wound up and ready to go.

Finishing his interview, Big Hal asked, "One last question Stalebread, what do you call your kind of music?" Stalebread answered emphatically, "It's called *hot music*. We play nothin' but hot music."

"Hot music," Big Hal repeated, bemused by the term. Stalebread punctuated his proclamation with his favorite call, "*Hot* cha cha cha cha!"

The audience roared with laughter when they heard this.

"You boys look like you're rip-roarin' and ready to go. I better get out of the way now!"

Big Hal swept his arm toward the band one last time, "Ladies and gentlemen, boys and girls: The Razzy Dazzy Band!"

The crowd at first applauded with reserve. They had already accepted Stalebread, because he was so charming, but their anticipation for god-knows-what drew only polite clapping. They knew these were newsboys by their garb and bare feet, but no one in the audience had ever seen newsboys in a musical band, and no one quite knew what to make of their odd musical instruments.

The band gathered around Chinee and his bass, at

center stage. Stalebread leapt up, playing his harmonica to kick off "Hot Time in the Old Town Tonight." This was a wise set-opener because the tune was a national hit at the time, and everyone knew the lyrics, so it guaranteed the audience would join in singing. The boys in the band enunciated every verse of the song, stepping to the front of the stage to be closer to the audience so people could not only hear the lyrics but could lip-read them, too. Almost immediately, the crowd was on its feet and stomping along.

> Come along, get ready wear your
>   bran' bran' new gown
> For there's gwine to be a meeting
>   in that good old town,
> Where you know'd everybody and
>   they all know'd you
> And you've got a rabbit's foot to
>   keep away the hoo-doo
>
> When you hear that the preaching
>   does begin
> Bend down low for to drive away
>   your sin
> And when you gets religion, you
>   want to shout and sing
> There'll be a hot time in the old
>   town tonight my baby
>
> When you hear dem a bells go
>   ding ling ling

All join 'round and sweetly
    you sing

And when the verse am through in
    chorus all join in
There'll be a hot time in the old
    town tonight.
There'll be girls for ev'rybody in
    that good, good old town,
For there's Miss Consola Davis and
    there's Miss Gondolia Brown
And there's Miss Johanna Beasly,
    she am dressed all in red...

Stalebread noticed a couple of prudish spinsters in the front row who were among the few still seated. Both remained in their seats with their hands on their knees. They winced when the song named names: "Miss Consola Davis," "Miss Gondolia Brown," and "Miss Johanna Beasly"—in Victorian times, naming women outright was inappropriate. Having some fun, Stalebread sang to these two spinsters for the wind-up of the song. His flirtatious attention clearly ruffled their feathers. He laid it on thick:

I hugged her and I kissed her and
    to me then she said
Please oh please, oh, do not let
    me fall
You're all mine and I love you best
    of all

> And you must be my man, or I'll
>   have no love at all.
> There'll be a hot time in the old
>   time tonight! My baby

Winking at them, he turned to the band and gave them the high-sign to begin the next number, "Rosie O'Grady."

The Razzy Dazzy Band's infusion of the Spanish tinge into all of the popular melodies was well received that night, as it had been in Shreveport.

Alternating between fast and slow tunes, Stalebread knew he'd want to finish with a medley that would get the audience on its feet one more time. There were no lyrics to this one—just raw energy from the international hit, the "Can-Can." It was made famous at the Moulin Rouge dance cabaret in Paris, with its line of dancing girls kicking up their dresses and showing off their petticoats. People knew of the Can-Can from poster and magazine illustrations. Now these boys were playing it in a chorus line and kicking up a storm, just like the Parisian girls. As their tumultuous stomping began, the audience rose with excitement, and children made their way to the aisles, to high-kick along with the band. That's when the two prudish women got up and left, apparently finding the raucous "Can-Can" the last straw. The Razzy Dazzy Band had this audience in the palm of their hand.

After the "Can-Can," Stalebread settled the crowd back down with his father's favorite song, "Maison Denise." This was followed by two lively Cajun songs, also sung in the French Creole dialect.

For their grand finale, Stalebread huddled with his band while the audience continued applauding.

"Okay, boys, we're going to go squirrelly with 'Whiskey in the Jar.' Don't forget those freezes, head bobs, and leaps—all them squirrelly moves you seen 'em doin' in the trees." The boys let out a "Hurrah!" and broke out of the huddle. Stalebread counted off the beat and they all began banging away on their instruments and singing with all their might.

> As I was goin' over
> The Cork and Kerry mountains
> I saw Captain Farrell
> And his money he was countin'
> I first produced my pistol
> And then produced my rapier
> I said, "Stand and deliver or the
>   devil may take ya."

Theatrically, the boys suddenly froze, looked around in suspended animation—as squirrels do—and Cajun, Monk, and Warm Gravy started their game of tag. Instruments were flailing and it seemed that Warm Gravy's original foreboding of impalement by bass fiddle might be in the mix after all. Stalebread, Family Haircut, and Chinee remained calmly in their places and continued the song without missing a beat. The audience was perplexed and engaged, as the boys froze in mid-flight and all of them stood in silence, alert, heads pivoting like squirrels. Suddenly the tables were turned and Stalebread, Family Haircut, and Chinee broke into a fierce game of tag, as

Warm Gravy, Cajun, and Monk held up the musical end of the chaotic choreography.

The audience howled with laughter. Limbs and instruments poked out in every direction from the cockamamie band, and made a hilarious sight, set to the song "Whiskey in the Jar." The lyrics fit perfectly with their antics.

> Musha rain dum a dog, dum a da
> Whack for my daddy, oh
> Whack for my daddy, oh
> There's whiskey in the jar

The audience had never seen anything like this but clearly enjoyed the spectacle. The children had never left the aisles and were now more worked up than ever. The band had another go at being "squirrelly" during the last verse:

> Being drunk and weary
> I went to Molly's Chamber
> Takin' Molly with me
> But I never knew the danger
> For about six or maybe seven
> Yeah in walked Captain Farrell
> I jumped up, fired my pistols
> And shot him with both barrels

The audience roared in appreciation. Stalebread faced them, saying, "Thank you, ladies and gentlemen, boys and girls. It has been our pleasure playin' here in the beautiful city of Jackson. We'll see y'all next time. Thank you very much."

The audience kept clapping and stood for an ovation. Some in the audience called out for an encore. Getting the nod from Big Hal, Stalebread looked out into the crowd, saying, "All right, thank you, thank you! Just one more before they give us the hook." He turned to the band and said, "'Froggy Went a Courtin',' boys!" This was another widely known song, giving the audience one last opportunity to join in singing. It ended their appearance on a warm communal note.

> Frog went a courtin' and he did
>   ride, uh-huh
> Frog went a courtin' and he did
>   ride, uh-huh
> Frog went a courtin' and he
>   did ride
> With a sword and a pistol by his
>   side, uh-huh, uh-huh, uh-huh

Big Hal Hallock returned to the stage clapping hard as the boys traipsed triumphantly off stage, disappearing behind the curtains. They stood backstage, bathing in the applause.

After the show, the boys hung around to schmooze, hoping to meet the magician—and especially his assistant. They looked for the man in black and his raven, but they had disappeared. The first person to approach the band was the well-dressed talent agent Colonel Boudreaux, who introduced himself, shaking each of their hands. The Colonel held six train tickets to New Orleans and six crisp dollar bills in his left hand, and waved them with fanfare before handing them to Stalebread and the boys.

"Gentlemen, if all y'all want to perform in Mississippi again, you just call me, hear?" Stalebread promised they would.

The Elks Lodge's caretaker had invited the boys to sleep at the Lodge that night. He swept up the floor while the boys folded chairs and stored them. When all was done, they spread out their bedrolls on the stage and settled down to sleep with their instruments. The caretaker wished them a good night's sleep and turned off the house lights.

As they tried to get comfortable enough on the stage floor to fall asleep, they recounted the night to each other, each throwing in a choice detail of the evening. Of all that occurred, in their eyes it was the old man in black with his eerie sounding saw and his rascally sidekick who took the cake.

"Even his eyes was black, like the raven's," Monk pointed out.

"The old man and his raven were like from another world," Stalebread said, "like they had come out of some dark swamp."

Chinee wondered, "Do you think the old man taught his raven to be a kleptomaniac?"

"Maybe that's their primary source of income," Family Haircut speculated. "I mean, he went right for the lady's diamond hat pin. That hat pin twinkled like it was worth somethin'."

Stalebread added, "He wouldn't have to train him much—ravens are natural-born thieves."

The boys drifted off to sleep, still talking about the old man and his raven.

In the morning, the boys woke up to the smell of coffee. The caretaker had reheated a big pot of leftover coffee for them.

"You boys were real good last night," he said, "never seen nothing like that stuff before. They'll be talking about your band around here for some time to come."

He sent them off that Sunday morning with their bellies full of leftover coffee and leftover popcorn. The band members thanked the man for his hospitality and set off for the train station.

On their way, the boys were recognized by a few locals who had been in attendance at the Elks Lodge. One boy about eight years old ran up to them with a homemade guitar he was working on. The boys gave him a few useful tips about the construction. A young couple walked toward them and the woman asked, "Say, what do you call that stuff you were playing last night? We really liked it."

"Hot," said her boyfriend, "They call it 'hot.'"

"Hot music," the boys said in agreement. Stalebread punctuated his answer with a "*Hot* cha cha cha cha!" The couple joined in the "*Hot* cha cha cha cha!" laughing at the funny salutation.

As the boys next passed two teenaged girls sitting on a porch swing, they waved at them and the boys waved back. A woman came out from behind the screen door and shooed the boys away with a look that could have curdled milk. The six young touring musicians continued their march through the quiet neighborhood toward Jackson's train station on West Capitol Street. They found empty benches to lounge on until their southbound train was ready to board. The engineer gave a little toot on the train whistle as the conductor put the steps in place for boarding passengers, and the conductor snapped open his gold pocket watch, loudly announcing, "All aboard for Crystal Springs, Hazelhurst, Brookhaven, McComb, Ponchatoula, LaPlace, Metairie, and New Orleans." The band boarded the southbound train, and once again had a coach to themselves.

Stalebread boasted, "Okay, boys, we really pulled it off! Two cities in a row makes a tour don't it?" They all laughed.

"Indubitably!" Family Haircut exclaimed.

"Indubitably!" Warm Gravy agreed. They all laughed, pointing at each other and saying, "Indubitably!"

They arrived back in New Orleans five hours later, a clear sky above. Approaching from the distance, their hometown sparkled in the sun.

"Dog-gone, but New Orleans looks good!" Stalebread said.

The band members made it back to the Newsboys' Home in time to attend the evening Sunday mass in the chapel. After mass, the other orphans wanted to hear all about the "Tour." The basketball game stopped and everyone present in the gymnasium surrounded the band, asking questions and demanding the boys draw out every story. Warm Gravy told them about the girls in Shreveport, and Cajun told them about the guys scowling behind the girls and how they all turned out to be pleasant after all. Monk told them all about the night train to Jack-son: "We each had our own cushy bench to stretch out on, and it was rock-a-bye baby all through the night." Chinee described the Elks Lodge event, and they all chimed in with details of the vaudeville acts. Stalebread told everyone about Colonel Boudreaux's open invitation. As evidence of their wages, each band member showed off their dollar bills and train-ticket stubs. Stalebread boasted that Colonel Boudreaux would book them whenever they wanted to return to Mississippi. "Anytime we want."

PART TWO
THE CAT CAME BACK

9. THE DISTRICT

We rag 'em all!
—Stalebread Lacoume

BACK IN NEW ORLEANS, THE BAND MEMBERS returned to their usual routines of selling papers and playing music. A change had taken place with the boys, though. Harassing the German Oompah bands no longer appealed. After having traveled "far and wide" in a matter of days, they lost all interest in those "hot battles."

The bandmembers met in the gym in the late afternoons as always, resting on the cool hardwood floor until the last of them gathered and they were again ready to head back out to the streets together for some musical "roving" before dinner. Their first stop was at the foot of Canal Street down by the wharf, where commuters crossed the river to Algiers. There was plenty of room for the boys to have a rollicking good time, and enough room to go "squirrelly" which amused commuters. By around six o'clock, the band would head back to the Home for supper. Old Mrs. Kelly made hot meals for the orphans and the half-orphans, who always got their ten-cents worth with her big portions.

From seven until nine, they would be in class on the second floor. At nine, off they went, back to Canal Street. They'd pick up where they'd left off and work their way up to the St. Charles Theater queue. After they worked that queue, they made their way up Canal to the New Orleans Passenger Terminal depot, simply referred to as the Depot. The train station always had a steady stream of sporting gents, tourists fresh off of the trains ready to spend money.

The band was on their usual nightly prowl up to the Depot one night when they came across a fraternity of ten young men in their twenties stepping off the train. The Biloxi Yacht Club dandies wore gold regatta pendants attached to their sky-blue blazers. Each gent was topped off in a straw boater hat. The Biloxians had just come in on the westbound Panama Limited and disembarked in New Orleans at the doorstep of the District, with the sole intent of indulging in some debauchery. The Razzy Dazzy Band played music for some of the Biloxi gents as they waited for the last of their young men to disembark. The revelers drank from hip flasks while The Razzy Dazzy Band serenaded them with hot music. The band called incoming tourists "fresh gents." "Spent gents" were the outbound tourists. Spent gents were easy to spot because they usually appeared hunched over, heads in hands, resting elbows on legs, looking dejected. The band never played for spent gents because, by definition, these men had no more money. On this evening, one spent gent wandered onto the train tracks trying to board an imaginary train. A patrolman had to rescue him from himself.

"Take me away, anywhere away from here," the repentant spent gent pleaded to the sky. He was escorted into a police wagon for his own safety. With quivering lips, he moaned repeatedly, "Anywhere but this circus!"

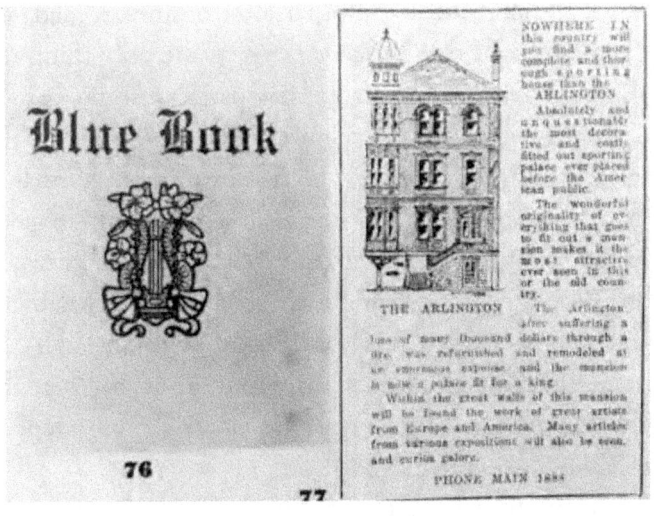

Tourist guide to the red-light district

The Biloxi Yacht Club members assumed that the boys playing music for them were intimately familiar with the District because they each had *Blue Books* to sell. The *Blue Book* was a thirty-page directory of the District that cost twenty-five cents; this was another source of income for the boys. The booklet primarily advertised saloons and bordellos and featured photographs of the lush palaces, their courtesans, and their matron proprietors. A madam's "'jolly good girls" posed in elegant gowns, lounging in some pictures and frolicking in others. The saloon advertisements pictured long bars bedecked with booze bottles, glass canisters of hard-boiled eggs, and jars of candied fruits, with beer spouts down the length of the bars.

The *Blue Book's* requisite photographs of the palatial exteriors ensured that tourists would recognize the establishments. Advertisements for drugstores, cigar manufacturers, bail bondsmen, and other local businesses made up the remainder of the *Blue Book*. It was the only thing the boys hawked up there, because newspapers just did not sell well at the Depot. Warm Gravy sold a *Blue Book* to the ringleader of the fraternity, who had introduced himself as Martin. As his fraternity brothers gathered around to gawk over his shoulder, the other band boys swooped in to sell more *Blue Books* to the others. Martin quizzed Stalebread about "points of interest" as he thumbed through the pages, and the bandleader answered as if he were an authority on the subject, despite never having stepped inside the District before.

Martin stopped at the two-page centerfold spread of Emma Johnson's Basin Street Mansion. There was an advertisement for Emma's Circus (which was Emma's code name for her dog-and-pony show). "We can pass on Emma's Circus," Martin said with a grimace at the thought of bestiality.

The Biloxi Yacht Club, all accounted for, numbered ten. For the rambunctious fraternity, the six musicians played a rowdy set of songs. Many of the band's tunes were popular and the club members joined in with the boys singing "Hot Time in the Old Town Tonight." Hip flasks were hoisted for toasts while the band played "Ta Ra

Ra Boom De Ay" and "The Cat Came Back." When the music stopped, club leader Martin officially offered the boys fifty cents apiece to serve as their guides into the District. The band, having a bit of fun with the Biloxi boys, accepted the offer.

For fifty cents each, the bandmembers played the roles of savvy street urchins. The Biloxi fraternity gents believed they would get their three dollars' worth out of the boys, and followed their young guides as they paraded through the District. The troupe of ten Biloxi fresh gents and six bandmembers proceeded down the line along the lake side of Basin Street. The Terminal Saloon, located behind the Depot, was the first watering hole they came upon.

"This joint is a tourist trap," Stalebread informed the gents. The boys guided their group past The Terminal Saloon, with Stalebread informing them, "It's lousy with pickpockets." Next door was another clip-joint, Few Clothes Cabaret, also crammed with tourists. The air inside was filled with so much cigar smoke it looked like river fog, and Stalebread suggested they skip this one, too. Their Biloxi employers, however, insisted on going inside because the name of the place clearly promised some exhibition of female flesh. Stalebread tried to explain to them that the name "Few Clothes" derived from the mispronunciation of proprietor George Foucault's last name, and it was just a ruse. "Cabaret" also bolstered the suggestion of can-can dancers. As there was no dissuading his Biloxians, he quit trying, but it was not long before they reemerged from the smoke-filled den, coughing and disappointed. They admitted to Stalebread that he was right after all. "There may have been a whole chorus line of naked women in there," Martin joked, "but, we couldn't see through the smoke, even if there was. Where to next, Stalebread?"

Tom Anderson, the District's unofficial mayor

The next establishment for the troupe was Tom Anderson's Fair Play Saloon. Tom had recently changed its name to solidify his business partnership with his girlfriend Josie Arlington, who owned Arlington's, her mansion two doors down Basin Street. The sign painter was in the middle of updating the lettering to read "Tom's Arlington Annex."

The establishment had not changed in any other way than its name. His system for his saloons needed no tinkering with. He plied the fresh gents with booze and directed them down the line to his paramour Josie's bordello. After she finished with them, Josie would point them back to Tom's for more drinks until they became spent gents. The Biloxi expedition continued down Basin Street one block, where they crossed Custom House. The boys led the Biloxi crew to Tom's doorstep. On especially busy nights like this, Tom would latch the two spring hinged saloon doors open wide.

Tom Anderson was the District's unofficial mayor, and the newsboys knew his story well. When he was their age, Tom had started out as a newsboy with a camp on Rampart and Canal. As a teenager looking to graduate into a new phase of his career, Tom's opportunity came one day while hawking papers at his camp. He witnessed a man carrying a black satchel out of a jewelry store, with a pistol in one hand. The suspicious fellow slipped into the alley. Young Tom quickly crossed Rampart and followed the man's trail into the alley. Tom saw the thief jump into a big, empty trash can, and hide under the lid. This odd spectacle was followed moments later by two well-dressed men from the jewelry store running out in pursuit. They also brandished pistols, and two beat cops ran up and joined them, all looking for the robber. As the four scratched their heads, Tom walked up to them and said, "Follow me."

Some of the many business interests of Tom Anderson, a supporter of the boys.

Tom Anderson's business card

The foursome followed Tom down the alley and he pointed out the trash can. Without further incident, the culprit was apprehended. A police wagon arrived at the end of the alley, and the thief was hauled away. One of the officers pulled out a notebook and pencil to interview their crime-buster. Tom offered to appear in court as a witness if needed, but as the jewelry thief was caught redhanded with the goods, he was informed that this would not be necessary. Nonetheless, the officer in charge patted Tom on the back and told him to keep up the good work. Tom took this to heart, and from then on, always kept his eyes peeled for trouble to report.

Tom's lifelong affiliation with the police department began that day. After that successful apprehension, Tom was rewarded with small stipends by the beat police who covered that territory. He became their eyes and ears—a "stool pigeon," he called himself. Tom Anderson eventually joined the New Orleans Police Department and was in time promoted to the rank of detective.

Tom Anderson retired from the NOPD at age thirty-four and opened his first restaurant and bar in the District on North Rampart Street. After terrific success, he opened another place in 1895 with a business partner, Billy Struve. Billy was a newspaper writer and also the publisher of the *Blue Book*. His office was on the second floor, above the saloon. Because of Tom's connections, the Fair Play Saloon was a perfect spot for the city's movers-and-shakers and also for on- and off-duty policemen. Tom's floor plan included a string of private booths perfect for clandestine meetings, and many back-room deals were made in these booths. The two banquet rooms in the back were available for stag parties.

Whether it was called the Fair Play Saloon, Arlington Annex, or Tom Anderson's Annex Café and Chop House, Tom's was always the place for cops and bigwigs alike, and as a result, Tom's political tide rose even higher. He was made a board member of the state lottery, receiving a handsome salary for his position. Tom Anderson became the arbitrator of local disputes, which was how he became known as "the Mayor."

Stalebread and his band escorted the young men of the Biloxi Yacht Club to Tom's saloon because they wanted to surprise Tom with their gaggle of fresh gents. Burly Tom was at the door when the troupe crossed the street, advancing toward him. He was pleasantly surprised watching these boys herd ten fresh gents into his establishment. The two swinging doors were latched open, offering the herd of stags a wider berth. Pied piper Stalebread escorted the pack through the entrance with the wave of his hand.

"Welcome, welcome, welcome," Tom greeted each Biloxi gent as they stepped inside his establishment. The other boys in the band all remained outside on the banquette, and lingered under the long awning as a rain cloud drizzled past. Tom came back out and introduced himself, thanking the boys for bringing him business.

Tom saw the boys' instruments and put two and two together. "You've gotta be those newsboys I've heard, The Razzy Dazzy Band. Listen, if you want to stand out here and play for tips, play, go ahead, play your hearts out, and feel free to come back anytime you want, boys."

"Yes sir, Mister Anderson," answered Stalebread, "We play hot music. Nothin' but hot music!"

Tom gave the musicians the lowdown. "The District's got Professors in every parlor, and pianolas[1] in every

---

1. The pneumatic-powered piano, or pianola required no musical talent

saloon, but nothing much in between. No hot band in the District, that I can tell you. Bands play standard stuff. I don't know any band who plays strictly hot. I like that. Say, I've got a hot 'Over the Waves' roll on my player piano right now, you hear that? First roll I bought for my pianola. I have one for 'My Gal Sal,' and a few others."

Stalebread told him, "We take all them popular songs and rag 'em. We don't pick and choose—we rag 'em all."

"You boys will go over big playing hot music around here," Tom told them. "Like I said, this banquette is yours any time you want to play out here. Be my guest."

Banquettes were raised wooden sidewalks along the District's muddy city streets. Under Tom's porch overhang, the band could stay out of the rain—and clear of the occasional emptying of a chamber pot from above. As the City Street Department progressed, block by block, the planks were repurposed and cement sidewalks replaced them. The canvas awnings stretched above the sidewalks, attached to buildings along every street. Any overhead covering, solid or canvas, made for an ideal place for them to play, giving them shade, protection, and amplification.

"Thank you for that offer, Mister Tom!" said Stalebread.

"You boys enjoy yourselves out here," he answered, and excused himself to go back inside.

The boys played for more than an hour outside the saloon, giving ample time for their Biloxi charges to spend

---

to operate. It took interchangeable rolls of songs, which was revolutionary, and contained a pneumatic or electro-mechanical mechanism that operated the piano action via programmed music recorded on perforated paper, or in rare instances, metallic rolls.

more money inside. They stopped playing when the fraternity brothers emerged. The liquored-up gents, prompted
by the salacious *Blue Book*, were ready to frolic in a Basin
Street mansion. Martin asked Stalebread which of the
eight bordellos on Basin Street he would recommend. Of
course, Stalebread and the boys took them a few doors
down to Josie Arlington's. In truth, any of those gilded
palaces along Basin Street would have served them well,
but Stalebread wanted to impress Tom's paramour by
giving her the fresh gents' business.

Basin Street bordellos resembled one another inside,
decorated from the marble floors to the vaulted ceilings to
impress their clientele. Crystal chandeliers, gold-framed
mirrors, landscape paintings, and Alfonse Mucha prints;
oriental rugs, and ornate tapestries featuring naked
goddesses were typical trappings. Gilded cages held exotic
birds. Cats routinely prowled the mansions, but the only
dogs in sight were the proprietresses' own personal pets.

The most beloved of all the bordello "pets" were the
men at the piano who were always dressed to the nines,
the "Professors." Depending on the mood in the parlor, a
Professor would either choose to be the center of attention
or keep a low profile, playing as if only for his own pleasure. The Professor was the prince of the parlor. Besides
being piano virtuosos, every Professor had to be a more
than competent singer and entertainer to get the whole
parlor singing along with them whenever they wanted to.

The working girls were the lifeblood of these establishments, of course. While some lived up to their advertised
beauty, some of the ladies made the men squint. Most of
them did not match the flowery promises extolled in the

Blue Book. To please their madams and their clientele, the average woman had to invest in exquisite apparel, transformative cosmetics and French perfumes to enhance what beauty they already had.

Martin and another Biloxi brother rang Madam Josie Arlington's doorbell and were thrilled to be greeted by Josie herself. To their delight, she looked just like she appeared in the *Blue Book*. After Josie gave them a tour, Martin came back outside and rallied the rest, "This place is swell, boys. Get on up here." He went down the stairs to settle up with Stalebread and the other newsboys.

"Josie is sure a swell gal. Mighty fine place she has, mighty fine! I knew you'd steer us in the right direction. We're all set for the rest of the night now, Stalebread. I guess we won't be needing your services anymore." He pulled out his coin purse and took out some silver dollars. Handing them to Stalebread, he continued, "You guys were worth the three-dollar investment. Here are a couple of extra dollars on top of that!" Martin shook each boy's hand. He bounded up the stairs to join his brothers inside Josie's.

It was past midnight. Dog-tired, Stalebread and Family Haircut walked to their houses and their four bandmates headed back to the Newsboys' Home. From that night onward, the District became a part of the band's itinerary. After playing at the Depot, they went down the line to play outside Tom Anderson's saloon as their final stop of the day.

10. Old Judge Bezou

You may be a band, but you're a spasm band!
—Judge Henry Bezou

WEEKS WENT BY WITHOUT CONFRONTATIONS WITH the German street-corner bands. The boys stayed out of trouble, but trouble eventually found them one evening as they busked outside of the Grand Opera House on Canal Street. The band had played this choice spot the night before, and the night before that, and on both nights they were shooed away by the theater's uniformed doorman. As usual, The Razzy Dazzy Band would disperse, only to reconvene and resume playing after the doorman went back inside. On this third evening, the doorman intended to make them wish they had heeded his warnings. He did not roust them; instead he went back inside and made a telephone call.

As usual, the boys began working the queue once the doorman went inside. A few minutes later, a middle-aged man in an overcoat joined the queue. His coat lapels were turned up and his Homburg hat tipped low. More patrons joined behind him, and more came up behind them. The band worked their way along the queue. When they were right alongside the man in the Homburg, he sprung on them without warning, startling the other patrons in the line. The boys instinctively defended themselves from this unprovoked attack. Cajun hit the man over the head with his cigar box guitar, flattening the man's Homburg. Stalebread punched him in the stomach with his fist while the others kicked him in the shins. The man was unable to defend himself against this swarm. As overwhelmed as he was, he did manage to unbutton his overcoat and reveal his dark-blue policeman's uniform. Upon seeing his uniform, silver badge, and brass nameplate, "Chief John Journee," the boys immediately stopped their punching and kicking. This momentary pause gave the chief just enough chance to blow his whistle, and he blew it loudly and repeatedly.

Before they had time to run, three more uniformed officers appeared. In an instant, the policemen nicked the six boys, holding each by the nape of his neck. The captured band members offered no resistance and awaited their fate.

Chief John Journee was much worse for wear after the skirmish. He used his handkerchief to stanch the trickle of blood he felt running down his temple. Not having a mirror, he made a mess of his forehead. He proclaimed, "You six ruffians are hereby charged with disturbing the peace, public nuisance, disorderly conduct, blocking traffic, striking an officer of the law, and resisting arrest." This litany of charges had a sobering effect on the boys. A horse-drawn police wagon drew up to the curb next to them. The Chief informed the six boys, "I've been putting up with complaints about you ruffians for far too long, and now your time is up. Take them away, men."

Police wagon, then called "paddy wagon"

The boys were loaded into the wagon and driven away. The clippety-clop of the horses' hooves echoed as the solemn captives were hauled downtown to the Second Recorder's Court. None of the boys had ever been arrested before, but they all were aware that no lenience was given to youth. In fact, the courts treated children as small adults. (There was no such thing as a juvenile court system and it would be years before the Society for the Protection of Children was founded.) The boys knew that jail cells were filled with criminals of all ages, and that children, just like adults, were expected to fend for themselves in jail.

The wagon stopped downtown in front of the two-story Egyptian Revival building that housed the Second Recorder's Court of the Second Municipal District of New Orleans. It was the lowest court in the land, known for handing down its judgments swiftly. The Second Recorder's Court was busiest at night, mostly with drunks, prostitutes, brawlers, pickpockets and other reprobates, while the Second Recorder's Court's daytime docket contained civil cases involving public health, mortgage disputes, and property seizures.

Usually, defendants waited on benches in the hallway of the small courthouse as the bailiffs watched them, but this was a particularly slow night. The benches were empty and the bandmembers were brought directly into the courtroom. Defense lawyers were rare in this night court because most defendants could not usually summon one on the spot, even if they could have afforded one. Defendants usually pleaded their own cases. Court clerks attended every court case, but on occasion, cases went unrecorded in the Second Recorder's Court. Sometimes the only written record of a case in this court would be found in a journalist's account. Newspaper journalists (also known as "court reporters") often napped in the back row of the courtroom, keeping an ear open for a good "Man Bites Dog" story. On this night, one such reporter was about to witness a most peculiar case.

The dejected friends were booked at the front desk, each giving his street name with his given name. Their leader went first:

"Stalebread. Emile August Lacoume."

The others came up in succession:

"Warm Gravy. Harry Gregson."

"Chinee. Emile Benrod."

"Family Haircut. Cleve Craven."

Last but not least, the brothers stepped up to the desk.

"Monk. Frank Bussey," said Monk.

"Cajun. Willie Bussey," said Cajun.

The transportation officer told the desk sergeant, "That's all of them, Sarge."

The desk sergeant replied, "They'll all be tried together. Take them in."

They were told to bring their instruments along with them, and the six boys were escorted into the courtroom.

Presiding over the court was the Honorable Judge Henry Bezou, known as a good man and fair judge. He had been elected to his position at the age of seventy-one. His advanced age provoked speculation about how long he would last. Judge Bezou still had his quick wit, but some of his other faculties were not so reliable. His eyesight was failing, as was his hearing, and his voice was weak. The old judge was always asking someone to repeat themselves, or someone was asking the judge to repeat himself. It was comical at times and trying at others, but nearly everyone who knew him was fond of "Old Judge Bezou," as he was affectionately called. If not for his generosity, these deficiencies would have prevented him from being seated in the first place. A few years later, Judge Bezou was impeached, not for dereliction of duty, or negligence of any kind, but simply for his own good. "Inability to fulfill and discharge his duties" was the official reason given.

Chief of Police John Journee, who had been the instigator of the night's fiasco, was determined to be in the
courtroom for the proceedings against his pint-sized
assailants. The Chief of Police was sitting by himself in the
fourth row patting the small wound on his swollen forehead with his handkerchief.

Black-robed Judge Bezou entered his courtroom, and
from his elevated perch was surprised to see the battered
Chief of Police sitting before him. They had long known
each other. Judge Bezou spoke down to John Journee.
"What's that on your forehead, Chief? Did you run into
something?" He did not care for Chief John Journee and
could not resist teasing him. Likewise, Chief John Journee
did not care for Judge Bezou, considering him not tough
enough on criminals. He had often heard complaints from
his police officers about how their cases against criminals
were thrown out by "Old Softy." In fact, there was some
truth in both their reputations: John Journee relished all of
his department's arrests, and Judge Bezou was lenient
when he could be; he would jail a drunkard if they were
too intoxicated to be set free on the streets and had no cab
fare.

Night in, and night out, the Second Recorder's Court
dealt with petty criminals, but Judge Bezou also dealt with
burglars, stick-up men, strong-arm thugs and the occasional murderer, so this judge certainly knew when to lay
down the law, and he did now.

Journee explained to Judge Bezou, "The little
scoundrels who are coming in next gave me this, and I
hope you give them a sentence they'll never forget. But I'm
not gonna bet on it with you, Old Softy."

The judge raised one eyebrow at the chief's insubordinate dig. Both men sat in silence. The judge closed his eyes and rested his chin on the palms of his hands as if napping.

When the Judge heard a commotion and opened his eyes, he found six young boys being escorted to the front of the courtroom. Some were holding contraptions that he could not identify. A few rows back behind them, Police Chief John Journee sat impatiently, still dabbing the cut on his forehead. In the back of the courtroom, a newspaper reporter slumped over his notepad. He perked up when he heard the boys come in and recognized them as The Razzy Dazzy Band. The reporter flipped to a fresh page in his notepad; he knew this was going to be interesting.

The court deputy stood before the bench to announce the boys' case: "All rise for the Honorable Judge Henry Bezou, presiding over the Second Recorder's Court of the Second District of Orleans Parish, in the Great State of Louisiana."

Judge Bezou took command of his courtroom by calmly tapping his gavel. The court clerk announced, "Court is now in session. Please be seated." Judge Bezou motioned to the court clerk, who recited the charges against the boys. The judge listened to their legal names and their colorful nicknames, and pondered the serious charges that had been read out. Judge Bezou repeated the charges, one by one: "Disturbing the peace, public nuisance, blocking traffic, disorderly conduct," and after pausing for a moment, concluded, "assaulting an officer, and resisting arrest. My, my," said the old judge, not quite concealing his chuckle. Judge Bezou looked over at Chief John Journee and raised one of his bushy eyebrows.

The reporter covering the proceedings sat in the fifth row, behind Chief Journee. He jotted his notes in shorthand.

"Who's the leader of this gang?" the Judge inquired.

Stalebread stepped forward and confessed, "It's me."

Their leader politely volunteered, "We're not a public nuisance. We're a band, Your Honor." Stalebread repeated, "We're just musicians. All we were doing was playing our songs when we were pounced on."

Old Judge Bezou was bemused by Stalebread's insistent claim. He was quiet for a moment before he broke his silence. "If you're a band, let's hear you play."

The reporter furiously composed his story.

The boys had their instruments with them: the cigarbox guitar, the soap box, the half-barrel bass fiddle, and the rest. Stalebread lined up his gang and slipped them the name of the piece. They were ready to play "Rosie O'Grady." When he gave them the high sign, they cut loose.

The band played while keeping their feet glued to the floor. They were not used to being so constrained, but this was clearly not the time or place to go all squirrelly. Even though the boys were restraining themselves, their energy filled the courtroom. Each boy bobbed and weaved his body in place while playing and singing "Rosie O'Grady."

Judge Bezou looked them over, weighing their fate. When they were finished, he had come to his decision and addressed Stalebread declaring, "Stalebread, you may be a band, but you're a spasm band! Discharged!"

Police Chief Journee fumed when the judge dropped all the charges against the boys. He stormed out of the courtroom with the newspaper reporter following behind. Outside the courtroom the reporter asked the police chief for an interview, but was immediately rebuffed. A minute later, the boys skipped out of the courtroom, fully exonerated and happy to talk to the reporter. They filled him in on the details that Chief John Journee wouldn't have dared to admit, recounting how it all started that evening when they were "leapt upon without warning."

The next morning, the orphans and half-orphans gathered in the gymnasium to hear the story firsthand from the six band members. The little kids were the most anxious of the congregation. These youngsters were Piggy Louis, Booze Bottle, and Seven Colors. This trio sold the early edition *Picayune,* and stayed as long as they could before they had to get their papers from the dispatch offices across Natchez Alley.

When the band's tale concluded, the boys hurled questions at them. Warm Gravy, Cajun, Monk, Chinee, Family Haircut, and Stalebread took turns answering.

Having left only minutes earlier, Piggy Louis, Booze Bottle, and Seven Colors came running back to the gym from across the alley waving copies of the early edition of *The Picayune,* yelling, "Read all about it! Read all about the Spasm Band!"

There on page three of the early edition was a headline in boldface: "Spasm Band Serenades Recorder Bezou."

Stalebread snatched a paper from Piggy's hand and began reading the news story aloud. The first paragraph detailed their arrest at the Grand Opera House, and the second paragraph detailed their appearance in the Second Recorder's Court. It was a brief but lively account that mentioned the band's "wild" hot style and portrayed the "spasm" band as triumphant, while Chief John Journee was portrayed as the instigator. The story ended with the dramatic courtroom scene and Judge Bezou's final declaration: "Stalebread, you may be a band, but you're a spasm band! Discharged!"

Stalebread fixated on the article, and while reading it over and over, he had an epiphany. The term "spasm band" was jumping off the page. Spasm was now their brand, and he embraced it. Old Judge Bezou not only gave the boys their freedom, but he also gave them the addition of "spasm" to their name, and lots of great publicity.

"Boys, listen up," Stalebread proclaimed. "From now on, we own spasm. See; we *are* spasm. And we make spasm music. From now on, our name is 'The Razzy Dazzy Spasm Band.' We are hereby a spasm band! Old Judge Bezou said so himself—it's right here in print!"

Stalebread's stroke of genius was confirmed with a mighty "Hurrah!" from everyone in the gymnasium.

11. THE RAZZY DAZZY SPASM BAND

You can't buy that kind of publicity, kid.
—J.T. Sullivan

The St. Charles Theater, one of the most prestigious theaters in America in the early 1900s

.   .   .

Stalebread wasted no time capitalizing on their publicity bonanza. He had his own copy of *The Picayune's* morning edition, waving the page-three story for all to see. Stalebread showed it to passersby who must have thought it was for sale, but he was waving it out of sheer delight. He would riff on the headline, "Spasm Band Serenades Old Judge Bezou!" The words rolled off his tongue.

One of those customers, theater promoter J.T. Sullivan, stopped at Stalebread's camp, and introduced himself.

"You're the kid I read about in *The Picayune* this morning, aren't you?"

Stalebread brandished his dog-eared copy, pointing to the headline, "You bet!"

The man smiled, saying, "You can't buy that kind of publicity, kid. Half the people in the city read that this morning."

This made Stalebread smile. Sullivan looked Stalebread in the eye and said, "I think I can help you capitalize on that." Handing Stalebread his business card, he properly introduced himself, "My name is J.T. Sullivan."

Stalebread listened intently, his mind racing with excitement.

"I'm scouting for a local act for next week's vaudeville review at the St. Charles Theater," Sullivan explained. "We had an act cancel on us this morning, Minnie Minnesota. Hot music's getting really hot right now. No vaudeville stage has hosted a hot band yet, but I've been thinking seriously that the. St. Charles should be the first. I heard a pit orchestra playing a hot tune during intermission last week. I think a vaudeville audience would really enjoy your Razzy Dazzy Band. I didn't even know there was a real hot band out there until I read this article. Your outfit, thanks to this article, is on everyone's lips this morning. I was just talking to the manager of the St. Charles, and he said he sees your band almost every day out in front of his place, and what's more, he enjoys you. I would like to offer The Razzy Dazzy Band a slot on our bill at the St. Charles next weekend."

Stalebread could hardly believe his ears. He shook Mr. Sullivan's hand, while politely correcting him, "That will be The Razzy Dazzy *Spasm* Band you're hiring. We call ourselves a spasm band now, 'cause of Old Judge Bezou calling us that last night. Yes sir, Mr. Sullivan, The Razzy Dazzy Spasm Band will be more than happy to be on the bill."

"Fine, fine, Son. Stop by my office, and we'll sign the paperwork. Can you come by later this afternoon? I'll be in."

"Yes sir, Mr. J.T.," Stalebread promised.

Stalebread could hardly wait to break the news to his boys back at the gym at the Newsboys' Home. By then, he would have a contract in hand as proof that he wasn't putting them on. After all, the St. Charles Theater was one of the most prestigious theaters in America at that time. They'd have a right to think he was smoking something funny. This would be the first time in history that a hot band was hired to play only hot music on a national stage. The boys knew the St. Charles was the big time. The theater had hosted such international superstars as Jenny

Lind, "'The Swedish Nightingale,"[1] and Lola Montez, creator of the world-renowned "Spider Dance."[2] The St. Charles was still attracting world-class talent at the time. The boys had every right to feel that they had "arrived." This was a monumental accomplishment, not only for The Razzy Dazzy Spasm Band, but also for hot music.

In preparation for the band's debut at the St. Charles Theater, Stalebread arranged for the band's formal portrait to be taken. Many professional photography studios had shops along lower Canal Street in the 1890s, and Stalebread made an appointment for his band at the Chas. Tyemi Studio. He told his band members, "The St. Charles management will put our publicity photograph behind their glass preview case out front, if we get it to them right away."

On Monday morning, the band converged at the Chas. Tyemi Studio at 9am. Mr. Tyemi unlocked the door, flipped his sign to read "OPEN," and ushered the kids and their instruments inside. The photographer was particularly charmed with the bass fiddle that Chinee carried. Mr.

1. Johanna Maria "Jenny" Lind (1820–1887) was a Swedish opera singer often referred to as the "Swedish Nightingale." One of the most highly regarded singers of the 19th century, she performed in soprano roles in opera in Sweden and across Europe, and undertook an extraordinarily popular concert tour of the United States beginning in 1850.
2. Marie Dolores Eliza Rosanna Gilbert, Countess of Landsfeld (1821–1861), known by her stage name Lola Montez, was an Irish dancer and actress who became famous as a Spanish dancer, courtesan, and mistress of King Ludwig I of Bavaria, who made her Countess of Landsfeld. At the start of the revolutions of 1848 in the German states, she was forced to flee, and emigrated to the United States, where she performed as a dancer and actress, one of her offerings being a play called *Lola Montez in Bavaria*.

Tyemi had them follow him to the backroom set, where his camera stood on a tripod in front of a small stage. Heavy curtains draped from the ceiling to the floor behind them, giving the illusion of opulence.

Photo of the Razzy Dazzy Spasm Band, taken at Chas. Tyemi's Studio on Canal Street in 1897

Mr. Tyemi had a composition in mind. First, he placed Chinee at the center of the stage, with the bass fiddle directly in front of the camera. Chinee stood poised with his bow across the strings, his left hand gripping the instrument's upper neck.

Once the band was posed, Mr. Tyemi rushed back to his camera.

"Not even a twitch." Tyemi warned them as he ducked under the hood and lit the flash. The Razzy Dazzy Spasm Band left their mark on jazz history with this formal studio portrait.

Two days later, the boys returned to pick up the prints. To their delight, their portrait was perfect and the prints were extra-large.

"Dignified, wouldn't you agree?" asked the proud photographer. They all agreed. The Razzy Dazzy Spasm Band delivered two freshly minted prints to the St. Charles Theater. A reproduction of their portrait was eventually published in an 1899 issue of *Railroad Trainman* magazine and the photo has since been reprinted in many publications over the years. It remains the only known photograph of The Razzy Dazzy Spasm Band.

Friday, the day of their first performance, the boys broke their newspaper routines and took the whole day off preparing for their show that night. They picked up their best shirts at the French laundry in the morning. In the afternoon, they took showers, and band members nervously groomed themselves until it was time to march over to the St. Charles Theater.

On the way to the theater, Stalebread took the opportunity to convey a pep talk, as if they were going into battle.

"This is the big time, boys. It don't get any bigger than the St. Charles Theater. Before that story in *The Picayune*, we were just playing the St. Charles queue. Now, we're on their stage. We got to deliver, boys!" They all understood.

"Got any tricks up your sleeve, Boss?" asked Monk.

Stalebread answered, "Well let's start out with 'Willie Tell.' That'll get the audience going, an' I been thinkin' it might be a good number to go squirrelly on, straight out of the chute. Give 'em the old one-two punch. Just when they catch on to what we're up to with the 'William Tell

Overture,' we'll go squirrelly! The stage is huge, and we'll have all the space we need to run around. Now, Chinee," Stalebread continued, coaching his bass player, "I want you to stay in your spot. I want you doin' that hesitation thing, where you just look around swivelin' your head and blinkin' your eyes. The rest of us will take turns playing tag. I want Chinee to be the steady beat, and two of us at all times playing with him. We'll tag-team and switch off a couple of times during the number. I'll give the sign when we wrap it up."

"That audience ain't gonna know what hit 'em," Cajun said.

Stalebread agreed, "Yeah, and we won't let up the pace either. Next we'll do 'Hot Time In the Old Town Tonight.' Everyone knows the lyrics to that one—heck, we may even get them rich folks singin' along."

"What else we playin' after that?" Cajun asked.

Stalebread reached in his pocket and pulled out a scrap of paper that contained their set list.

"Besides 'Willie Tell' and 'Hot Time,' there's 'Rosie O'Grady,' "Cat Came Back,' 'Over the Waves,' 'La Paloma,' and 'The Daring Young Man on the Flying Trapeze.' For our encore, you know what we'll do? We'll play 'Jesse James,' and just gallop right off the stage like a three-legged horse. That'll be a hoot!"

During the weekend of their vaudeville engagement, The Razzy Dazzy Spasm Band performed as the star attractions in three evening shows and two matinees. As planned, the band opened each performance with their madcap rendition of the "William Tell Overture." Audiences always laughed along with the kooky arrangement of the famous piece. Stalebread's family, Jennie, Emma, and Jimmy, came to each performance.

Attending one of their Saturday matinee performances was minstrel show impresario Doc Mulney, whose White minstrel show was booked to play for five days at West End Park on Lake Pontchartrain. After the evening show, Doc Mulney introduced himself to the band. It was common for minstrel show owners to scout for talent wherever they went, because they wanted to enlist local musical acts in the towns along their traveling route. Doc was always on the lookout for local talent to play in his oleo. The oleo was the middle segment of a minstrel show, in which local acts were featured.

Doc pitched his offer to The Razzy Dazzy Spasm Band, promising fair wages and "No blackface required. If you want to cork up, that's up to you. I don't make no one cork up. You can work in my Oleo anytime we're back, just as you are. I think your newsboy getup is perfect. I'll let you know when we're coming back and I'll book you boys." Doc handed Stalebread his business card and held out his program and a fountain pen so Stalebread could write down his phone number.

As promised, the band was included in Doc Mulney's oleo when his minstrel show came back the next time. They played in Doc's oleo whenever he returned with his traveling minstrel company.

At the St. Charles' shows, most people in the audience knew of The Razzy Dazzy Spasm Band. They'd already been popular around town before the newspaper article. The large stage was underutilized by all the other vaudeville acts in the revue, but the boys were used to performing under the sheds and knew how to make the most of a large space. This brought out their acrobatic antics, and audiences loved the spectacle. Chinee's flashy trick was spinning the bass fiddle on its endpin. He'd glued a tiny mirror on the backside of the instrument. Each time he rotated the bass, the mirror reflected the footlights, creating a dazzling effect. It was a twinkling star at the center of The Razzy Dazzy Spasm cyclone, while the other band members traded off on lead and back-up vocals by jumping out front. At each show, the band received the loudest applause of any act of the weekend.

The street-urchin newsboys captured the audience's attention, including those in the front rows, filled by well-to-do patrons, many from the Garden District, the toniest residential area in New Orleans. After each of The Razzy Dazzy Spasm Band's performances, the boys were approached by people wanting to meet them. On Sunday night, an elegantly dressed couple introduced themselves after the show and inquired about the band's availability for a private party the next Saturday afternoon. Mr. and Mrs. Rivard from the Garden District offered the boys a silver dollar apiece to perform at their debutante daughter's birthday party. Stalebread graciously accepted.

The following Saturday afternoon, the band showed up at the Rivards' Garden District home on St. Charles Avenue at three o'clock, as requested. They were instructed to come to the back gate of the Greek Revival mansion. This debutante affair was a sweet sixteen party for young Deborah Rivard, who was celebrating in style with twelve of her friends.

The boys' shirts were fresh, which was only appropriate

considering everything at the Rivard's home was pristine, right down to cheerful rows of white daisies that lined the Corinthian-columned wraparound porch. Their starched white shirts made them presentable. They were greeted at the rear gate by a uniformed servant named Geoffrey who brought them into the backyard and showed them up to the spacious porch. As they sat on cushioned wrought-iron chairs around the matching glass table, Geoffrey went inside for a moment and returned with a crystal punch-bowl, and a maid followed behind him with a platter of petit fours and pralines. Geoffrey insisted they help them-selves and said he would fetch them when it was their time to perform.

A few of the debutantes peered out the windows at the boys. "I wonder if they are housebroken?" one of them joked. The other girls giggled.

The platter was empty by the time Geoffrey returned for the band, so the boys gathered their instruments and followed him into the residence through the kitchen door. The gaggle of teenage girls and Geoffrey escorted the band into a small ballroom that he called "the conservatory."

Mr. and Mrs. Rivard came in and welcomed the new arrivals.

"Daddy and I discovered The Razzy Dazzy Spasm Band last week at The St. Charles' Variety Night. We know you will really enjoy them."

From the moment they stepped inside the Rivards' home, the boys had been staring wide-eyed at everything. Never had any of them been inside such a lovely place, or seen such a lovely gathering of girls. The walls were tall and the ceilings high.

With a wave of Stalebread's hand, the band jumped into action, opening with their breakneck version of "Willie Tell." The giggling girls poked each other, daring the bravest of them to begin dancing. After the first began, the other girls followed suit. The debutantes showed off their improvised moves, imitating the boys' prancing. The band demonstrated the shimmy, the duck walk, and other funny moves for the girls to try out. Their hot music was infectious, and Deborah's parents enjoyed the syncopated frolicking from a safe spot behind the grand piano.

The Razzy Dazzy Spasm Band played for a full hour until they and everyone else ran out of steam. All the band members were younger than the girls, too young for the girls to be self-conscious over, leaving the coquettes feeling at liberty to mingle and flirt with the boys. Naturally, the band members adored the older beauties in their pastel gowns.

When it was time for the party to play "Pin the Tail on the Donkey" and other parlor games, Geoffrey came for the boys and escorted them out the same way they had entered. At the back gate, he handed them each a shiny silver dollar and extended a paper bag filled with more petit fours and pralines.

"You boys were splendid," Geoffrey said, as they left the yard. He locked the gate behind them.

The Razzy Dazzy Spasm Band played many more debutante parties in the Garden District over the years. One day, while walking home from one of those Garden District parties, the boys discovered a little park with a manicured lawn in a newly developed downtown district. It was on Baronne Street facing the two newest theaters in the city: the Tulane and the Crescent. The park instantly became the band's favorite place to play outdoors. It provided a carpet of grass that the sprinkling system made glisten. Shade trees surrounded the park. The pedestal drinking fountain gurgled with cool water. They couldn't have asked for more.

The park had been created out of a small lot that had served as a construction yard of the contractor. The contracting company was obligated by the city to make it nice after building the Crescent and Tulane Theaters. The band adopted it as their own. The boys, as if stewards of this bit of paradise, referred to it as "our park." The sprinkler system supplied the drinking fountain, and the boys liked to put their thumbs over half of the faucet to spray each other. The birds and squirrels liked to bathe in the puddles.

They played music there regularly, earning generous tips from the upper- and middle-class pedestrians who strolled by. The grand opening for the two theaters took place in the early fall of 1898 and the Razzy Dazzy Spasm Band was there waiting to entertain the theater crowds.

They continued making their nightly runs up Canal Street to the District, still their last stop of the day. Being the only hot band performing in the District on the street corners, they weren't about to abandon their stake. The band's two favorite spots were polar opposites and literally as different as night and day. The afternoons in their park were bucolic, and at night in the District, danger was always afoot. Avoiding trouble was half the fun.

12. Olga Nethersole

She smiled and bowed and blew me a kiss.
—Stalebread

Theater magnates Abraham Lincoln Erlanger and Marc Kraw became business partners in New York City in 1888, where they quickly revolutionized the nationwide contract and booking aspect of the theater business. By the 1890s, the two impresarios were the most powerful men in American theater. In 1898, they completed the Tulane and Crescent theaters in New Orleans as the crown jewels of their burgeoning empire. The side-by-side sister theaters across the street loomed large above the little park where Stalebread and his band liked to play. During their construction, massive amounts of concrete were poured for foundations, steps, ramps, walkways, and the 30 by 90 foot expansive promenade between the theaters, called the "Arcade." The city also poured concrete sidewalks for foot traffic around the properties, defining the perimeter of the park.

The boys frequented their park in the late afternoons when it was more inviting and leisurely than the rush hour foot traffic on Lower Canal Street. They found that their music was more appreciated by the birds, squirrels and passersby than by the homeward-bound commuters anxious to catch their streetcar or ferry.

Directly across from the park was the wide marble staircase ascending to the Arcade. Spanning the arcade, light-bulb letters spelled out "The Klaw-Erlanger Co. Theaters." The buildings' façades and the length of the arcade were festooned with more than a thousand incandescent electric lights. The red, white, and blue bulbs could be programmed in three hundred and thirty-six different lighting combinations, and many pedestrians strolled by at night just to enjoy the mesmerizing display.

Though the exteriors of the sister theaters looked exactly alike, their interiors served two different clienteles. The 1,800-seat Crescent, on the left, was the theater for the common folk. Melodramas, comedies, musicals, and minstrel shows were presented to satisfy popular taste. The Crescent, with its polished brass fittings, was not as plush as its sister theater, the Tulane, where everything was gold-plated. The 1,500-seat Tulane was as opulent as the finest European theaters and appealed to New Orleans' posh patrons by staging classics, originals, operas, Greek tragedies, comedies, Shakespeare plays, all with the big stars of the day. The Razzy Dazzy Spasm Band played their music in the park, benefiting from the affluent theater traffic.

The highlight of the theater's 1899 inaugural season was the arrival of world-famous English stage actress Olga

Nethersole, who was scheduled to make her first appearance in New Orleans. Her two-week run at the Tulane began with Arthur Wing Pinero's *The Second Mrs. Tanqueray,*[1] described as a shocking and controversial drama about a "woman with a past." Olga's reputation as a performer preceded her. In advance of her arrival in New Orleans, she made a big splash with her four productions in Chicago and St. Louis.

The boys in the band were well aware of Olga's stardom, as the newspapers frequently ran stories of her international scandals. Heralding her arrival was a large lithograph poster of Olga in costume behind glass outside the Tulane. The boys walked over to gawk at the poster the first day it was displayed. During Olga's run that fall, four different posters featured her in different costumes as she switched roles. Stalebread was particularly smitten by her after catching a glimpse of the star when she first arrived in the city. After watching her get out of a carriage near the rear stage exit door, Stalebread ran back to the park, insisting to the others they all attend at least one of Olga's performances together.

The first of her four theatrical offerings, *The Second Mrs. Tanqueray,* would have been fine with the boys, but they were turned away by a gruff box office manager, who told them that they were too young, and added snobbishly, "Besides, you whippersnappers are filthy."

---

1. *The Second Mrs. Tanqueray* is a problem play by Sir Arthur Wing Pinero. It adopts the "Woman with a past" plot, popular in nineteenth-century melodrama.

Stalebread immediately retorted, "We may be dirty, but we're never filthy, mister."

International theatrical producer, performer, and star Olga Nethersole

Olga's second production was Sir Arthur Wing Pinero's *Profligate*. It was a sordid and grim domestic melodrama that ended with a horrific suicide. Once again, the boys were rebuffed by another Tulane staffer at the ticket booth when they tried to buy tickets.

The third production in her two-week run was just as provocative as the first two: Alexandre Dumas' *Camille*.[2] As her friend Sarah Bernhardt had done, Olga played the lead role of Margaurite, the original "'tart with a heart." Her stage kisses were notorious for being "long, deep, and passionate," and that popular stunt led a New York theater critic to coin the term "the Nethersole Kiss."

After *Camille* debuted at The Tulane, one local columnist gushed about the actress' reception in the city, writing, "The fashionable audience rendered a 'verdict' of absolutely unqualified approval upon Olga Nethersole's presentation. New Orleans approved completely of the new star."

Another local theater critic swooned, "The furor Miss Nethersole has caused is genuine and New Orleans has not been so moved in favor of an actress since the days of [Sarah] Bernhardt. The success of her engagement must be regarded as simply astounding." Bolstered by the scandalous publicity surrounding "The Nethersole Kiss," *Camille* sold out before the boys could even come up with a scheme to get tickets. Time was running out for them when she launched her last production, *Sapho*,[3] which she

---

2. Alexandre Dumas fils (27 July 1824 – 27 November 1895) was a French author and playwright, best known for the romantic novel *La Dame aux Camélias* (*The Lady of the Camellias*), published in 1848, which was adapted into Giuseppe Verdi's opera *La Traviata* (*The Fallen Woman*), as well as numerous stage and film productions, usually titled *Camille* in English-language versions.

3. *Sapho* was a 1900 American play by Clyde Fitch based on an 1884 French novel of the same name by Alphonse Daudet and an 1885 play by

also produced and directed. Stalebread was determined to get his boys to see the fabled Olga perform. For this "problem play," having to do with a "loose woman," the boys knew they would be turned away again and wondered who could help them.

Sapho tickets were scarce, and were being scalped at astronomically high prices, due to the trial centered on her *Sapho* production in New York City. Seven months earlier, Olga, her co-star Hamilton Revelle, manager Marcus Mayer, and Wallack's Theater owner Theodore Moss had been arrested in New York; the scenes depicting a confident woman having affairs with married men led to charges including offenses against public decency, and creating a public nuisance. Playing a courtesan was not the subject of the trial so much as the revealing costumes and lurid language. The unspoken issues provoking the moralists were how Olga's character challenged the norms of gender, intimacy, and sex.

Rancor against Olga was stoked by entertainment industry men who resented her role as a producer. Her staunch advocacy of women's rights and her robust intellectual independence were also reasons behind the establishment's public condemnation. Undaunted by any of this, Olga bolstered the spirits of her fellow co-defendants. Their two-day trial resulted in a jury needing just fifteen minutes to acquit the production's personnel, proving that long-dominant Victorian morals were finally losing sway

---

Daudet and Adolphe Belot. The play was not an exceptional success but is considered a notable step in the transformation of American society's attitudes regarding gender roles and public depictions of sex in the 20th century.

in America. Olga shrewdly used her trial publicity as a springboard to launch her current American tour. When the newsboys read about her trial, they felt a kinship with the defiant Olga. After all, they had their own run-in with the law following some of the same charges.

Before, during, and after Olga's trial in New York City, she was the object of even more press attention than usual. She had learned from her mentor Sarah Bernhardt about creating headline stories as fodder for the society pages. Tantalizing stories about Olga circulated from New York City around the world. While hawking newspapers, Stalebread and his crew turned anything Olga-related into a headline-shout, no matter if it was a front-page story or a small mention inside.

"Extra! Extra! Read all about it!" they'd shout, with special glee, "*Olga's triumph in court!*"

"*Olga rallies support for women's suffrage!*"

"*Olga shops at Tiffany's!*"

"*Olga does it again!*"

"*Olga's kiss!*"

"*Olga! Olga! Read all about it!*"

The band had little hope of seeing Olga's upcoming show, but as time was running out, Tom Anderson came to their rescue, giving them six tickets to *Sapho*. Stalebread had appealed to Tom a week earlier and, in the nick of time, he came through. "Second Row, stage right," Tom pointed out.

On the evening of the performance, the boys wore shirts that came back from the French Laundry starched as stiff as could be. Shoes were spit-shined. The fact that they were kids attending one of the most controversial plays of the season made them uneasy. The boys knew they were conspicuously underdressed, so they banked on the shirts and the spit-shines to make up for all they lacked.

On their way to the theater, Stalebread halted his troupe in front of a florist a block away from the Crescent and Tulane theaters. He quickly returned with a dozen red roses bound by a green satin ribbon and adorned with a bow.

To hide the bouquet while he was in line, Stalebread held it behind his back. The crew of six shuffled along in the slow queue.

Tulane theatergoers were always dressed to the nines, and while the boys thought their clean shirts and polished shoes helped them fit in, they knew they'd better keep their fingers crossed. At the entrance, two uniformed ticket-takers tore their tickets into stubs without looking up, and the boys passed through the checkpoint without incident. Once inside the crowded lobby, they convened at a water fountain, hardly able to contain their glee.

They marveled at the fabulous interior decorated in Louis XV style. A captivating 22 by 16 foot oil painting commanded the lobby that featured fairies driving chariots in reckless abandon across a road of clouds, with attending cherubs playing instruments in glorious Rococo splendor. It was like something from a dream. The boys lingered in the lobby, staring wide-eyed at the painting until ushers went around ringing small bells to signal the patrons to take their seats.

The boys made their way down the far-right aisle, hardly able to believe their good fortune for the evening. The bandmembers slid into the second row to the right of the orchestra pit, with Stalebread taking the end seat. Stalebread cradled the bouquet in his lap.

The immense stage was over sixty feet wide and over forty feet deep, far grander than that of the Crescent theater next door. The massive curtain sat ten feet behind the stage footlights and featured a huge illustration of a renaissance painting depicting the goddess Psyche at the feet of a semi-nude Venus. They gazed up at the colossal curtain in awe.

The house lights dimmed and the orchestra members took their places. Sheet music was shuffled on music stands and instruments were tuned. The conductor finally arrived and mounted the podium. He tapped his baton and the orchestra's gentle strains began. All chit-chat ceased when the massive curtain parted to reveal the fantastic set.

The play began with a scene in Dechelette's ballroom. Blue spotlights illuminated the masked dancers, who twirled like dervishes. When Olga made her entrance, she was welcomed with great applause. When the ballroom scene concluded, the audience rose from their seats in a standing ovation. As the massive curtain began to close for a change of sets, Olga stepped just behind her mark on the floor so that when the curtain closed, she instantly vanished from sight. The audience's applause grew even louder. Catching her breath, she waited for their enthusiasm to hit a crescendo before reappearing from behind the curtain. It was a well-practiced ritual between Olga and her audiences, and when she stepped to the front of the stage to receive their accolades, the audience's enthusiasm was as climactic as it would be at the end of the play, so keyed-up were they by the theatrical devices and her star quality.

This frenzy inflamed Stalebread, too. His bandmates noticed he had been busy with a spool of fishing line he'd pulled out of his pocket. They were puzzled at first, but when they saw him attach the end of the line securely above the fat ribbon that bound the roses, they poked and nudged each other, realizing their leader had something rascally in mind for those roses.

While the audience was still applauding, Olga took bow after bow, relishing the audience's reception. Stalebread stood up with the bouquet in one hand leashed to the fishing line in his other hand. When he stepped into the aisle to get a clear shot at the stage, the boys slunk down deep in their seats. They shielded their eyes with both hands, but peeked through their fingers to witness the scene. Stalebread stood like a pitcher on the mound, winding-up for the pitch before sending the bouquet flying over the orchestra pit. The bunch of roses landed right at Olga's feet. She saw the bouquet coming from the aisle to her left and saw the boy in the aisle jumping up and down and waving to her. Olga looked directly at him and threw him a kiss, and in response, he turned his cheek to catch it. It wasn't the infamous "Nethersole kiss," but it was enough for him.

As Olga kneeled to retrieve the bouquet, Stalebread gave the fishing line a good tug and the bouquet jerked away from her. The movement of the big bouquet startled her, and the audience let out a collective "Ohh." This prompted a wave of laughter from the audience, and Olga, never one to miss an opportunity to have some

fun, moved toward the animated bouquet to see what
would happen. Detecting the fishing line, she fully anticipated its next move, and played along by reaching for it
again. Stalebread gave another tug on the line and the
bouquet jumped away from her. This sent the whole
audience into hysterical laughter, which she thoroughly
enjoyed, as did its instigator. Olga and Stalebread
continued their charade, with her scooting and chasing,
and him pulling and teasing. They could have kept this
up were there more stage to work with. Finally, Stalebread let Olga grab it and she untied the fishing line
from her prize. The star of the stage waved it
triumphantly over her head, causing the audience to rise
to their feet again with thunderous applause. She
launched one more kiss that Stalebread caught with his
other cheek, then slipped through the curtain to prepare
for the play's second act.

The boys sat down as they watched Stalebread return
to his seat while winding his fishing line back onto the
spool. A moment later, two ushers strode down the aisle
and motioned to the six boys. In silence, the boys got up
and submissively left their row. They were led up the aisle
toward the lobby, where they were dealt with by the
theater manager. He chewed them out, assuming that they
were all in on the prank. Without further ado, the boys
were tossed out of the theater with the admonishment to
"Never come back to this theater again!"

Outside, the boys gathered around Stalebread. "Why
didn't you wait till the end of the play?" They all wanted to
know. "Now we've missed the rest of the play."

Stalebread apologized. "Honestly, I was planning on

waiting till the last encore of the last act, but I just got caught up in the frenzy."

Stalebread felt bad about getting them thrown out of the theater and had an idea to make it up to them. "Let's wait around back at the stage door to greet Olga after the play is over. I'll write her a note and see if the doorman will give it to her." Stalebread convinced his crew to go with him.

The boys were fine with his plan, though none shared his confidence that anything would come of the effort. Just the same, they proceeded to the stage door at the rear of the Tulane Theater. Warm Gravy had a stub of a pencil. The boys searched their pockets for some paper, and agreed that the piece Family Haircut produced was the best one.

"Dear Olga," Stalebread said as he wrote, "we would love to meet you here after the play. Signed, The Bouquet Boys."

They knocked on the stage door and a kindly old doorman opened it.

Cutting to the chase, they handed him their note and asked if he would take it to Olga. To their delight, he had a twinkle in his eye when he winked and accepted it.

The boys settled themselves nearby to wait for the play to end. About an hour later, the doorman held the door open for Olga. A vision of loveliness, she was unaccompanied, save for the roses, which she cradled in her arms. The boys rushed over.

"So you boys thought you would have some fun at my expense," she said with a smile, "but it seems it was at your expense. These theatre owners don't have a sense of humor, but I do, and it was all in good fun. I enjoyed our little charade immensely, and clearly my audience did, too."

Stalebread stood before her and the other boys flanked him. Olga continued, now talking to Stalebread directly.

"You should have seen how apologetic the house manager was for the 'accident.' I assured him that it was all in good fun and that it was actually the highlight of the evening. I've never experienced anything quite like it."

"You sure were a good sport, Miss Nethersole," Stalebread replied, "I should have waited till the end of the play to let loose, but I got carried away in the moment."

As the boys all nodded in agreement, Olga could not help but notice that some of them were holding what looked to be small stringed instruments.

"Are you some kind of band? Will you play for me?" she asked.

More than happy to oblige, Stalebread asked her to choose a song.

"Oh, do you know 'The Daring Young Man on the Flying Trapeze'? That's my favorite."

"We certainly do!"

"But we play everything hot," Chinee spoke up to warn her. "We get pretty wild with our stuff."

She was curious, "Well, let's hear how you perform my favorite song."

The boys took a few steps back and began to play. The sound was peculiar, but Olga was delighted to hear them play and sing all of the verses. She could not resist joining in, and they had a jolly time singing together.

When the song ended, Olga apologized for not being

able to stay with them longer. "I must get back inside to congratulate my fellow performers one more time before they leave."

The boys understood and were in the midst of their thank yous when she did something none of them could have anticipated in their wildest dreams: she invited them to visit her later at her hotel. She gave them her hotel's address, and told them to check in with the concierge when they arrived.

When they arrived at the hotel, Stalebread let the concierge know they were there to see Miss Nethersole, just as she had instructed. The front desk clerk called her and she came down to collect the ensemble. The boys and Olga had a great time playing music in her suite while she accompanied them on the baby grand piano.

The party lasted beyond midnight, and while she interacted with each one of the boys, she took a special interest in Stalebread. He was, after all, the instigator of the stunt with the roses. In their short vaudeville performance, a length of fishing line bound their friendship.

During the evening the boys spent in her hotel room, they discussed a gamut of topics between songs, including the state of the boys' education. Olga seemed to relate to Stalebread as if they were old friends, and she took him aside to talk to him. Olga had an intuition and recommended a local school that specialized in business skills, run by Miss Sophie Wright. Olga told him she would like to contribute to his education, and said she would pay his tuition.

"Sophie White is a friend of mine," Olga told Stalebread while the other boys swapped jokes in the main room. "She has a night school that now takes in male students. I will enroll you in her night school if that interests you. I think you will do well learning business there. Somehow I just know you'll like it."

Stalebread had been attending night school at the Home like his bandmates, but the thought that Olga would care so much that she would offer to pay his tuition made him accept her offer. True to her word, Olga arranged everything with Sophie White. Olga was his guardian angel, as far as he was concerned, and she kept in close contact with him over the years. Although they would speak often on the phone, it would be many years before they would again come face-to-face.

13. Hot Everywhere

Blowin' up a storm.
—Louis Armstrong

New Orleans' atmosphere was a perfect incubator for the birth of jazz. Orchestras large and small followed Captain Payén's habanera lead.

On a large scale, full orchestras played in the many parks along the shores of Lake Pontchartrain. Thousands of people attended huge outdoor events. Audience numbers were inestimable, considering everyone within earshot were potential audience members. This also included people far beyond the lake-front neighborhoods. When a full orchestra played there, it was reported that the sounds carried four miles into the city.

Among the small orchestral formations of five or six musicians were the German Oompa Bands. The German immigrants mainly played for tips on downtown street corners. They could only be heard about two or three city blocks away on a noisy day downtown.

Though the Razzy Dazzy Spasm Band had the same number of musicians, their inferior instruments could only be heard at close range outdoors. This didn't matter to the boys, whose spectators came near to put tips in their hat. The Razzy Dazzy Spasm Band's precocious charm and their antics attracted their audiences. That's when they passed the hat.

Other varieties of hot music emerged in the 1890s. Ragtime, the piano-driven sensation with its jaunty lilt, was complex, sophisticated, and the antithesis of spasm. It was popularized by the publication of sheet music, and especially by the advent of the pianola in 1895.

Pianolas championed ragtime music and vice versa. Like sheet music, player piano rolls were sold in stores and mail-order catalogs all over the world. Scott Joplin, a piano teacher from Sedalia, Missouri, began publishing his own songs in 1895. Within a few years, Joplin embraced ragtime, and wrote his own "rags." In 1899, he penned "The Maple Leaf Rag," which remains one of ragtime's most recognizable tunes. His other huge hit, "The Entertainer," served to lift Scott Joplin out of obscurity. Ragtime fell out of favor within his lifetime. He predicted it would eventually return to popularity but didn't live long enough to be able to say, "I told you so" when a new generation rediscovered him in the early 1970s.

The habanera craze that began with Hart's publication of the *Mexican Series* sheet music never lost its original audience of "reading" musicians. Among the aficionados were professional orchestra members playing in the theaters. These theater orchestras were paid to play what they were hired to play, yet during their intermissions they began experimenting. Eventually these hot flings during intermissions led to music directors adding hot arrangements to their repertoire.

John Robichaux was a New Orleans musician and bandleader who balanced his work between two different disciplines. He was playing the bass drum in the hot Excelsior Brass Band, while also leading his own society band, The John Robichaux Orchestra.[1] His orchestra played at high-toned establishments such as Antoine's Restaurant. John began adding hot touches to his traditional repertoire by inserting cakewalks and ragtime numbers as early as 1897, and even more frequently by 1899. Meanwhile, his little orchestra was still playing conventional waltzes, quadrilles, mazurkas, two-steps and schottisches, their stock in trade. Among his contemporaries who blended genres were Adam Olivier's Band and The Silver Leaf Orchestra.

By the late 1890s, many New Orleans bands were reworking tunes with habanera beats—so much so that hot was no longer considered cutting-edge. What was novel in the late 1890s was being forged in brass by a "non-reading" musician who hailed from Uptown, the cornetist Buddy Bolden.[2] Buddy brought the raw power of

---

1. John Robichaux, sometimes spelled Robechaux (1866–1939), was an American jazz bandleader, drummer, and violinist. He was the uncle of American jazz pianist Joseph Robichaux. He moved to New Orleans in 1891, where he was the bass drummer for the Excelsior Brass Band from 1892 to 1903.
2. Charles Joseph "Buddy" Bolden (1877–1931) was an American cornetist who was regarded by contemporaries as a key figure in the development of a New Orleans style of ragtime music, or "jass," which later came to be known as jazz.

the blues into hot music. This self-taught cornet player's hybrid style became known affectionately as "Gut Bucket." It was forged in the heat of the rough Uptown dancehalls. Most notorious among the Uptown joints was Union Sons Hall at 1319 Perdido Street. Inside the hall, Buddy and his band worked dancers into a slow-grinding sweat with their hybrid of blues and hot music. People started calling Union Sons Hall, "'Funky Butt Hall," referring to the lack of ventilation and the body odor within. Buddy played Gut Bucket for couples grinding with hips shaking. He infused his magic into secular songs including "My Bucket's Got a Hole in It" and "Turkey in The Straw." Gospel songs also were fair game for Buddy's treatment, with such songs as "Ride on King Jesus," "Go Down Moses," "What A Friend We Have in Jesus," and "Nearer My God to Thee." He also transformed the popular songs of the day, like "Ida," to his liking. Buddy dug deep when he wailed straight-up blues, playing tunes like "If You Don't Shake You Get No Cake," "Careless Love," and "Make Me A Pallet on The Floor." Buddy's self-penned "Funky Butt" and "Get Out of Here and Go Home" were his show-stopping numbers.

Bolden was notorious for how loud he blew his horn. It was said that when he played along the banks of the Mississippi River, his horn could be heard in Algiers. In his autobiography, Louis Armstrong recalls living on Jane's Alley down Perdido Street from the single-story Funky Butt Hall. "Buddy Bolden was blowing up a storm," as Armstrong put it. Like young Louis, the orphans in their top-floor dormitory of the Newsboys' Home just a little further down Perdido Street could hear Buddy Bolden, too. His inventions live on, though he was never recorded. Joe "King" Oliver and other devotees of "King" Bolden carried on his sound and it still predominates in New Orleans and beyond.

Furthering the spread of hot music on another front were the elite musicians known as Professors. This specialized group of New Orleans entertainers were accomplished pianists who sang and played everything and anything requested of them. The Professors entertained the wealthy clients and courtesans of the classy bordellos. They were the highest-paid musicians in town. Professor Tony Jackson said his tip jar only knew two denominations: "twenties and hundreds."

After their evening shifts in the mansions, the Professors would often play until sun-up in some spittoon saloon.

One of the most industrious Professors was the prolific Clarence Williams (the songwriter of "Cake Walking Babies From Home," and dozens more). Clarence was a savvy businessman and cofounder of the Piron & Williams Publishing Company. He also ran his own joint that stayed open so late they served breakfast. Clarence is credited with creating The Ham Kick, a saloon sport in which women competed for a ham suspended from twine, the winner being the woman who was able to kick high and hard enough to drop the ham. The women could throw as many kicks at the ham as they wanted. Clarence had the hams dangle at a calculated height to ensure maximum upskirt exposure. It was a real crowd-pleaser. The Professors could entertain both high-class and lower-class clientele, all in the same day, and were welcomed everywhere. Some were even pimps themselves, like Jelly Roll Morton. Jelly Roll, who called himself "Winding Boy," became the most famous of the Professors from New Orleans by traveling the country propagating the Spanish tinge. As Jelly Roll used to insist, "Of course you have to have these tinges of 'Spanish' in it, in order to play real good jazz."

Professor Tony Jackson, the Man with a Thousand Songs

In those days, the Professor of highest esteem was the dapper Antonio "Tony" Jackson Jr., who penned the hit song "Pretty Baby." He was called the "Man with a Thousand Songs." "What am I supposed to tell a customer when he puts a twenty in my jar and requests his favorite song?" Tony would say. "'Sorry, I don't know that number?' Why, I have to know every song, every song there is."

Six years older than Jelly Roll Morton, Tony Jackson was a mentor to the younger man, though Morton liked to say he was self-taught. Morton, known for his ego, claimed that he was "the best," but in rare moments of humility acknowledged Tony as the greatest of them all.

Jelly Roll Morton, world-famous New Orleans Professor

Jelly Roll bested Tony only once, when the two were paired against each other in a public "duel" in Chicago. Gamblers made bets on the outcome, with the odds on Tony to win. Jelly Roll went first, giving an impressive performance. At the conclusion, he stood up and accepted the crowd's applause before relinquishing the bench to Tony, who came over to sit at the piano. Jelly Roll sidled up behind Tony and whispered into his ear, "You can't play. You can't remember the lyrics." Tony stumbled during his performance and Jelly Roll beat the odds and won. Jelly Roll later said he had hexed his opponent with the old voodoo curse called "seeds of doubt." After he admitted to this supernatural trickery, Jelly Roll declared that Tony was indeed the "Best in the Land."

When Tony left New Orleans for Chicago, he shared his wealth of hot material and innovations widely. Tony drew large and appreciative audiences in the Windy City. He was the toast of Chicago, but after having spent years playing in the intimate settings of Basin Street bordellos, the big-time nightclub scene of Chicago proved to be overwhelming for Tony's mild-mannered, effeminate personality. He returned to New Orleans both mentally and physically broken. Tony loved booze, but it led him to an early grave.

The importance of New Orleans marching bands can't be overstated. Marching bands in New Orleans have historically provided the heartbeat for all of the city. These bands, known for their John Philip Sousa material, could be heard approaching long in advance of their arrival, and were heard long after they passed by. Sousa, an American composer of Spanish descent, was accomplished and prolific, rising in status to become conductor and arranger of the "President's Own Marine Band" at the White House in the late 1880s. A trained violinist, he had written more than 100 military-style marches, and his celebrated band toured for decades around the world. While Sousa's band played with its traditional 4/4 beat, other marching bands converted his pieces to habanera beats, poetic justice, as Captain Payén's military band introduced habanera to the United States in the first place.

Black communities had their own marching bands, and played the same type of engagements as their white counterparts, which were funerals, picnics, parties, parades, processions, and political rallies. African-American marching bands are renowned for playing in funeral processions. Those bands are hired by men's benevolent societies that honor their recently departed dues-paying members. The marching bands leading the funeral processions to the cemetery are trailed by mourners in what is called a "Second Line," a glorious procession for their guest of honor. On the way to the cemetery, the bands play a "slow drag" dirge that dramatizes a prolonged arrival at their final destination. Conversely, on their return from the cemetery, the pied pipers lead the celebrants in an exuberant, parasol-twirling celebration of their dearly departed's life. With joyful high-stepping, they play, "When the Saints Go Marching In," which is the predominant Second Line "return" song.

The most prestigious of the African American marching bands in the late 1890s were the Onward Brass

Band[3] and the Excelsior Brass Band.[4] Notably, Manuel Perez, previously of the Onward Brass Band, went on to form the Perez Imperial Orchestra,[5] which emphasized Buddy Bolden's influence.

Papa Jack Laine's Reliance Brass Bands[6] were the premier white marching bands in New Orleans. Jack always had one or more marching bands going at a time, and during Mardi Gras, often as many as seven at a time. Consequently, he employed more musicians than any bandleader in the city. From New Orleans' pool of talent came and went Laine's rotating musicians, Stalebread among them. People called Jack Laine "Papa" because he had so many musicians working for him in so many different Reliance bands over the years. It was a family

---

3.　The Onward Brass Band played often in its early history at picnics, festivals, parades, and baseball games. By 1887, it was under the leadership of Joseph Othello Lainez, a cornetist. Among the group's members were Isidore Barbarin, George Filhe, Lorenzo Tio, Peter Bocage, George Baquet, and King Oliver.

4.　The Excelsior was founded in 1879 by Théogène Baquet, who led it until 1904; following this it was led by George Moret (1904-1922) and then Peter Bocage, who led it from 1922 until its dissolution in 1931.

5.　The Imperial Orchestra was founded by cornetist Manuel Perez, and it operated from 1901-1908. Perez (1871-1946) was born into a Creole of Color family of Spanish, French and African descent. One of his ancestors was an officer of the free black regiment which fought in the Battle of New Orleans. Perez was known for his beautiful tone, staying close to the lead, while King Oliver improvised variations as a second cornet part.

6.　George Vetiala "Papa Jack" Laine (1873-1966) was an American musician and pioneering band leader in New Orleans in the years from the Spanish-American War to World War I. He was often credited for training many musicians who would later become successful in jazz music.

business, with his mother feeding the musicians and even letting them sleep on her floor during Mardi Gras.

It's no wonder that Jack recruited Captain Payén's star saxophonist, Florenzo Ramos, to play in his primary Reliance band. Jack Laine was twelve years old when Payén's Mexican Eighth Cavalry Band first came to the World's Industrial and Cotton Centennial Exposition in 1884. Jack's first instrument was a snare drum left behind by a Mexican musician. His father bought it for him at a pawn shop. Many fledgling musicians in New Orleans purchased instruments once pawned by Payén's Eighth Cavalry members. Many years later, Jack was proud to employ the venerable saxophonist Florenzo Ramos.

Before the end of the century, hot music had as many flavors as a New Orleans snow-cone stand.

Papa Jack Laine's Reliance Band, the premier brass band in New Orleans

14. Blindsided

Hard to believe a doctor could make such a mistake.
—Rose Weaver Lacoume

By 1900, The Razzy Dazzy Spasm Band had been one of the best-known bands in New Orleans for many years. Stalebread was fifteen years old and so was Warm Gravy; Chinee, Cajun, and Monk were fourteen; and Family Haircut was the oldest, at sixteen.

All the band members were seeking adult jobs, ready to bequeath their newspaper camps to the younger orphans from the Home, who had been substituting when they played music. As soon as they found the right job, the older boys relinquished their camps. Like Jack Dup and Tom Anderson before them, the band members were at the age when it was time to move on.

Warm Gravy knew being a musician would not be his profession. Like his idol, Tom Anderson, he was attracted to working in the police force. Warm Gravy's career path followed that set by Tom. Over time he attained the rank of Captain of Detectives, just as Tom had.

The American Boy's Handy Book, precursor to the *Boy Scout's Handbook*

Stalebread, on the other hand, had no doubt that he would continue making music professionally for his entire life. He had learned to play piano, guitar, banjo, and to expand his versatility he added harmonica, and zither.

Stalebread was a good singer and always had been, but when puberty caused his voice to break, his voice changed for the better.

Stalebread had not planned to formally break up The Razzy Dazzy Spasm Band, but they all knew the original lineup could not last forever. Stalebread approached three young orphans from the Home about becoming permanent replacements. Seven Colors had always wanted to take Warm Gravy's place in the band when the time came, and Seven Colors suggested his best friend, Emile "Whiskey" Benrod for Family Haircut's spot. Stalebread chose Whiskey to take over his camp, as Whiskey had already shown himself to be a reliable substitute and all-around good fellow. Family Haircut let Stalebread know that he would soon begin working in his father's barbershop full time as his family expected. His grandfather had opened the Tip Top Barbershop in 1866, and his father had taken it over in 1890. Family Haircut was the Tip Top's heir apparent. The third orphan Stalebread enlisted was young Piggy Lewis, who would replace Family Haircut on the paper-and-comb and singing through a stove pipe. Stalebread also promised to include his little brother Jimmy, whom he dubbed "Blameless."

Stalebread had no qualms about the changing roster; that was to be expected. But he was sentimental about his original compatriots, and in honor of their longstanding camaraderie, he planned something special to commemorate his crew: a camping trip.

These city boys had never been camping before, but they had Warm Gravy's dog-eared copy of Daniel C. Beard's *The American Boy's Handy Book*, and they daydreamed about camping, especially after reading the chapter "How to Camp Without a Tent." Beard had stirred their imaginations with flowery passages like, "The wonderful cottage of boughs, thatched with the tassels of the pines, was there ever a cottage out of a fairy tale that could compare with it?" The author's accompanying pen-and-ink illustrations made his fanciful constructions vivid and practical. Beard provided instructions for framing the structure and thatching the roof, and went so far as to suggest building add-on rooms and making furniture out of sticks and boughs. Stalebread's camping trip plan was embraced by all of the boys. They read, "The next best thing to really living in the woods is talking over such an experience."

They did indeed talk the camping excursion over for weeks, relishing their city-boy daydreams of adventures in the wilds of nature. One night at the Depot, on a magazine rack, they found a postcard of the Milneburg Resort, a campground on the southern shore of Lake Pontchartrain on a property surrounded by reassuring alligator-proof fencing. On the back of the card was a list of the resort's attributes, including woods, lakeside dock, fresh drinking water, latrines, and hot-water showers.

The train known as the Smoky Mary ran from the riverfront along Elysian Fields Avenue and around Lake Pontchartrain to the Milneburg Resort. They had finally found the perfect destination and decided to embark on their adventure on the following Thursday morning.

That day, the campers arrived at the terminus with bedrolls slung over their shoulders and instruments in hand for their first venture out of the city together since

1897. The boys bought their round-trip tickets just before boarding and let out a great "Hurrah!" when The Smoky Mary pulled away from the depot. The north-south tracks ran parallel to the old shell road that had once been an Indian trail. The outskirts of the city ended abruptly at a vast cypress swamp that extended to the shoreline of Lake Pontchartrain. On a clear day, you could see all the way from New Orleans across to Mandeville. The Smoky Mary chugged through the swamp, finally reaching Milneburg Resort. The campground and resort had expansive views of Lake Pontchartrain. A breeze off the lake greeted them as they drew near. The train stopped at the resort and the campers let out one more "Hurrah!" Stalebread went to the office and registered for a campsite. With their permit, they had their choice of the campsites, as none were all occupied. They chose a shady site near the lakeshore.

The campers waited to swim, because they first needed to construct their "cottage," which they did, following Beard's *Handy Book* instructions.

The six campers high-stepped over the alligator-proof fencing to forage for wood. Each of them wore his shoes on this camping trip. They paired off to gather enough wood for their structure. When they finally had what seemed to be enough, they heaved their bounty over the low fence. Stalebread was the last to leave the woods, right behind his partner, Monk. Before returning to the fence, he spied a long branch that he just had to have. Stalebread waded ankle-deep through ivy to retrieve it, while Monk waited for him on the other side of the fence.

After the hunt, they built their shelter, which took the greater part of the afternoon. Warm Gravy had *The Amer-*

ican Boy's Handy Book bookmarked at the chapter "How to Camp Without a Tent." Each boy had his own pocket knife, and they stripped branches and stacked them in a pile. Once the shelter was framed with poles, they followed Beard's instructions on thatching the structure.

When their hut was finished, it was time for a cool swim in the lake. None of them knew how to swim, but that didn't matter. They spent the late afternoon dog-paddling around the shallows. Again and again, everyone jumped off the pier feet-first and climbed back up the wooden ladders.

For dinner they went to the resort's dining hall; after dinner, the boys built a fire in the campfire pit. Stalebread surprised his crew with a bag of marshmallows that he had stuffed into his bedroll. The campers whittled skewers, roasted marshmallows, and sang cowboy songs under the stars until they had sung and played every cowboy song they knew.

Next they told ghost stories. Family Haircut narrated one in which a baby gets dragged into the swamp by an alligator and is horrifically eaten, and its ghost comes back to haunt the campground. As he ended the story, Family Haircut hushed the boys, whispering, "Listen… can't you hear it crying?"

Cajun told a spooky tale about a haunted pirogue that let its passenger paddle it out into the swamp and tipped itself back and forth until the passenger fell overboard, leaving the passenger to drown. The pirogue then drifted back to the shore waiting for someone else to take it out into the swamp, only to dump them overboard, and so on. This story could have gone on indefinitely, but Cajun stopped it after three victims. The boys finally turned in around ten o'clock.

The next morning, almost everyone woke up to the sunrise, thanks to a neighboring rooster. Stalebread had fallen asleep, but was awakened in the middle of the night by excruciating pain. His left eye was burning from the toxic resin of poison ivy, which he had contacted on their scavenger hunt for boughs.

At sunrise his companions discovered Stalebread huddled in the fetal position, weeping. When he rolled over and raised his head, they saw that one side of his face was inflamed. One of his eyes was bloodshot and his eyelids were also red and swollen. Stalebread had clamped his teeth onto his handkerchief to keep from screaming. The pain made him shiver uncontrollably. His bandmates huddled around him and took turns trying to comfort him. He could not talk, only whimper and cry.

The boys panicked. Chinee ran off for water, which was all they could think to use. Their unanimous decision was to end the vacation immediately and take that morning's train back into the city for medical help. Stalebread spent an excruciating two hours before the early train pulled out of Milneburg for New Orleans. The Smoky Mary seemed to move as slow as molasses getting to the city, and when it finally pulled in to the terminal, the boys could hardly wait for it to come to a full stop before jumping off. Family Haircut held Stalebread's right arm and shoulder and Warm Gravy held his left.

"We're gonna step off the train, boss. You let us do the heavy lifting. Just come along for the ride."

Stalebread nodded that he understood, went limp, and

allowed himself to be carried. His head fell forward and the boys suspected he had probably passed out. Family Haircut and Warm Gravy carried him to the "good" side of Basin Street. The river side of Basin Street had no bordellos but rather an array of ground-floor offices, including a bail bondsman, a dentist's office, a small drugstore, a Chinese laundry, and at last, the doctor's office they had sought. There were two doctor's offices, actually. The first general practitioner they found was a Dr. LaRose. His name was spelled out across the storefront window in gold leaf letters with black outlines. An Open sign hung from behind the oak door's plate glass. This prompted Chinee, Monk and Cajun to barge in. Family Haircut and Warm Gravy turned sideways to fit through the door with their limp leader.

In the waiting room, Cajun rang the bell on the small secretary desk to summon help, while Monk knocked loudly on the only other door in the room. When no one appeared, Chinee shouted, "Hello?"

Family and Gravy were cradling Stalebread on a couch when the doctor in his white coat opened the door with his shoulder, while drying his hands under his armpits.

"I'm Doctor LaRose," the man said brusquely. "What's all this commotion? What is it that couldn't wait?"

Family and Gravy pointed to Stalebread, who was lying between them. The doctor stepped up and inspected him closely, shining a flashlight at the swollen eye.

"Good you got him here, boys. This young man is in shock. His body has reacted to severe pain." Stating the obvious, his diagnosis was, "Bad infection in that eye." As the doctor looked into Stalebread's good eye, he concluded, "He's unconscious, but it's only temporary. He will come to soon, and when he does he will be in even greater pain than before. I will give him a small dose of laudanum now, and when he comes to, he will stay conscious."

The doctor went into his back office, and returned with a four-ounce amber-colored bottle fitted with a rubber-domed eyedropper. "The pain might well last for days. Now, watch me so you know how to give this to him later. This dose will wear off in a few hours. Be ready to give him one eyedropper full when his pain returns."

The doctor demonstrated how to put the eyedropper under Stalebread's tongue and administer the laudanum. The doctor held the bottle between his thumb and index finger and displayed it as he abruptly said, "Two dollars!"

The boys were surprised by the doctor's immediate concern with the bill, but they reached into their pockets and paid him.

"Thank you," the doctor said as he took their money, now lifting Stalebread's chin to get a good look at the boy's eye. The side of Stalebread's face was swollen from eyebrow to cheek, and his streaming eye had soaked the breast of his shirt with tears. Dr. LaRose let Stalebread's head rest back on his chest, and he stepped toward the boys.

"Poison ivy," he declared, "can ruin an eye for good. But, fortunately, I have just the thing for it. It's good you brought him directly to me, for I am the only one who has it for sale—I mean for treatment." Reaching into his coat pocket, he continued, "In this bottle, is a curative distillation. As we speak, it is awaiting its patent. It is a miracle cure for this insidious toxin that is torturing your friend.

Its ingredients I cannot reveal, but there is more than a hint in its name: 'Dr. Rose's Rosewater.'" The fancy label portrayed Lazarus being cured by Jesus. The bottle was made of frosted pink glass and sure enough the liquid was pink, too. Dr. Rose instructed the boys that the patient's affected eye would be soothed with a half a teaspoon of the tincture every two hours. "The swelling should subside by tomorrow evening."

Dr. Rose offered the bottle with his outstretched arm, but when Chinee reached out to receive it, the doctor pulled it back.

"Three dollars, please."

The boys amassed the additional funds and paid for the medicine. Before handing them the bottle, Dr. Rose administered an application himself by raising Stalebread's head and facing it upward. With the eye-dropper, he bathed Stalebread's eye in this curative, which ran down his cheek. "Like that. Every two hours, even through the night!"

The boys carried their miserable comrade out of Dr. Rose's office. Warm Gravy held the two medicine bottles in his hands and looked at his pals. "Any of you guys think this rosewater is really gonna work?"

Family Haircut was the first to speak. "Looks like fu-fu juice from the barbershop. Like lilac aftershave."

"I think the guy is a quack," said Monk, "but that Laudanum did the trick. He's been sleeping like a baby. Listen to him snore. Shh, listen he's snoring! That's a good thing."

Cajun agreed, "Just like a baby."

The boys debated what to do next.

"Where should we bring him?" wondered Warm Gravy aloud.

Chinee noticed that two doors down was another doctor's office, and he pointed. "Hey fellas, maybe we should bring him there."

The boys agreed. None of them were in favor of waiting to see whether Dr. Rose's Rosewater would work.

They led Stalebread to the office of Dr. Javis, whose office window had lettering just like Dr. Rose's. They entered the waiting room through the front door and gathered, waiting to be greeted. When no one appeared, they made a small commotion and as in the previous establishment, a white-smocked doctor appeared from a back room. This was Dr. Javis, his name embroidered on the smock. Dr. Javis was a handsome man in his thirties who could have been mistaken for a leading man of the theater, were it not for the thick lenses of his glasses, which made his eyes look absurdly large.

"What have we here?" he asked the boys when he saw Stalebread's condition. "Oh my Lord," he said, after taking a closer look at Stalebread's swollen face. There was compassion in his voice. While he was not the huckster that Dr. LaRose was, the boys smelled alcohol, but not the alcohol one usually finds in a doctor's office.

"Bring the patient! And follow me."

Family Haircut and Warm Gravy carried Stalebread into the back office and laid him on Dr. Javis' examination table.

"Thank you, boys," the doctor said, dismissing them as he opened the dusty window blinds to cast light onto the table and the patient.

Warm Gravy and Family Haircut took their cue and rejoined their comrades in the front room. There were not enough chairs for all of them, so Gravy and Family plopped themselves onto the floor, leaning their backs against the wall.

All were deep in their own thoughts. Only occasionally did one of them think of Stalebread's mother, but they were in a doctor's office across town. Surely, they figured, his mother would appreciate their resourcefulness in getting him treated right away.

The clock on the wall ticked loud enough to add to their anxiety. Fifteen minutes went by.

"I guess the doctor is a good one," said Monk, pointing to the framed diplomas and certificates on the wall.

"Princeton on one of those." Monk said.

"Where's Princeton? That sounds familiar," asked his brother.

"It's up north," Warm Gravy said.

"New Jersey," Chinee chimed in.

As more time passed without a word from the doctor, they started wondering what was taking so long. It was supposed to be an examination, and a half hour seemed like a long time for just that. When forty-five minutes had elapsed, they could no longer take the suspense.

"Come on, boys," Warm Gravy said, "let's go back and see what's taking that doctor so dang long."

The boys went into the surgery and saw Stalebread lying face up on the operating table, sound asleep. A large gauze pad covered the entire upper portion of his face. What completely took them by surprise was finding Dr.

Jarvis looking out the window and drinking from a flask. When he turned around, they could see he was despondent, with tears flowing down his cheeks. Most evident to them all: he was drunk.

"Wrong eye. Good eye gone. What to do? Laudanum, more laudanum? Ach, I'm so sorry!" He continued mumbling nonsensically, and seemed to be apologizing profusely through his drunken haze.

The boys were speechless. The doctor they had entrusted to examine their friend, the handsome doctor with all of the diplomas and certificates on the walls—was now standing there, a drunken mortal. An empty syringe lay on a small table next to a vial containing white powder.

When the boys turned their attention to their helpless comrade, one of them lifted the large gauze pad from his face. They gasped at the sight of Stalebread's bad eye, even more inflamed than before, as was the whole side of his face. But the most shocking sight was beneath the second smaller gauze pad that covered his "good" eye. Family Haircut lifted that pad to bear witness to what the doctor had done. Some turned away with revulsion, but none escaped the grisly truth that Dr. Javis had taken it upon himself to operate, without anyone's consent, in a drugged and drunken stupor, on the boy's good eye, which now looked to be an awful mess. Dr. Javis had rendered his poor patient permanently blind.

Outraged and distressed, a few of the boys gathered around their leader, who was in a drug-induced sleep. Family Haircut, Warm Gravy and Chinee positioned themselves once again to take all the weight of Stalebread's limp body. They ignored the stupefied Dr. Javis as they lugged their friend out of the office, in shock.

The brothers Cajun and Monk stayed behind, though. They looked at each other, nodding. The brothers approached the oblivious Dr. Javis. Cajun and Monk beat the irresponsible doctor with a vengeance before leaving him on the floor moaning for mercy.

Once outside, Cajun and Monk rejoined Chinee, Warm Gravy, Family Haircut, and their leader. The botched operation resulted in the immediate loss of Stalebread's good eye. Meanwhile, the inflamed one was getting worse by the hour, and his sight in that eye was completely lost, too, before the dreadful day was over. When Stalebread finally regained consciousness, he would learn the ghastly truth that he no longer had his precious eyesight. He would forevermore be in the dark. Stalebread's catastrophe should have been cause for Dr. Javis' license to be revoked, but there is no record of any punitive action taken against him for the irreversible damage he inflicted that day.

15. RECOVERY

A place for everything, and everything in its place.

SOON AFTER STALEBREAD WENT BLIND, JENNIE MOVED the family from their original residence on Exchange Alley to another French Quarter residence at 935 Bienville Street, number 7. The 1900 census recorded the Lacoume family members at this address as: Jennie: 41, widow, theatrical performer, head of household; Emile Jr., 15, newsboy; Emma, 12, at school; and James, 9, at school. Stalebread continued to pay for his siblings' tuition at St. Philips Elementary School from his savings.

The French Opera in New Orleans always had its ups and downs, including bankruptcy during the economic panic of the 1890s, but by the late 1890s, the company was again profitable. Despite having been away from the stage for fifteen years, Jennie was once again employed in her profession as a French opera singer, and the timing could not have been better.

Those first weeks of blindness were pure hell for Stalebread. The laudanum doses were effective, but they kept him suspended in a stupor. He was living in a black void where his blindness wore away his joy. He subsequently found himself battling depression and anxiety in those early months of his affliction, and his mother and siblings did everything in their power to keep his spirits up. Sleep was his only relief from all that weighed on him, but his family's love kept him from becoming despondent. Emma and Jimmy came home from school every day and the three of them played games. They told him every detail of their day, and this became the highlight of his day. Olga called him once a week on the telephone to help keep his spirits up, too. Band members also called him often. They all loved to reminisce about their glory days and that always lifted his spirits.

Dr. Bernstein, New Orleans' preeminent general practitioner, whom Olga had retained for Stalebread, incrementally weaned Stalebread off the laudanum he had become dependent on. This helped him with his withdrawal symptoms, even though every bone in his body constantly felt like it was being crushed until the ordeal was over. Gradually, Dr. Bernstein's patient became pain-free and regained a clear head. Fortunately, his balance improved and he no longer had the disorienting sensation of floating he had been experiencing for months.

Stalebread's first accomplishment in his newfound sobriety was feeding himself. Going to the bathroom on his own, washing his hands and face, combing his hair, and brushing his teeth were difficult, but he was determined to become as self-sufficient as he could be, as quickly as possible. It took discipline and perseverance.

Jennie used Father's straight razor to shave his bewhiskered face. The straight razor was the only thing Stalebread was unwilling to try using on his own. "I'd butcher my face if I tried that," he said.

Venturing on his own outside his bedroom had been a challenge, but with his regained balance, he began walking around the apartment unassisted. A month into his rehabilitation, Stalebread had his mother rearrange the furniture into obstacle courses throughout the day. Without the help of a cane, he was developing his proprioceptive sense, albeit with some bruised shins along the way. His mother offered to buy him a white cane, but he refused the offer. She suggested using Father's walking stick, but he declined that, too. He told her he would prefer not using a cane at all.

Stalebread had no qualms about wearing dark glasses, however. While the cane carried a stigma, "Sunglasses are snazzy," he told his mother. Jennie bought him a handsome Italian pair from Maison Blanche. It pleased him to hear the frames were gold-plated and that the lenses were iridescent blue. "The glasses were made in Venice. They look like shimmering blue butterfly wings," she told him. From that time forward, Stalebread wore his sunglasses during his waking hours. They gave him more confidence.

A few months of hesitant walking gave way to a slow gait. He never again regained the jaunty stride he had once possessed. His first full year of blindness was spent primarily indoors playing music all day, but by the start of his second year, Stalebread tested his navigational abilities in the streets, walking Emma and Jimmy to St. Philips School on Dauphine Street. His challenge was to return home by himself, and he eventually became comfortable with the journey. When walking home alone, he was often stopped by well-wishing friends, fans, and strangers for conversations. Stalebread gratefully accepted helping hands when he crossed streets, and he appreciated the kindness that allowed him to make his way around the neighborhood safely without a cane.

To get outdoors more often, Stalebread started picking up Emma and Jimmy after school, and the three siblings always took their time getting home. Some days they walked to the edge of The French Quarter to bask in the hubbub on Canal Street. Even blind, Stalebread felt at home in the familiar currents of Canal Street, exhilarated by the soothing hustle and bustle. The sounds and smells of the streets were his elixir. Thanks to his indomitable spirit, the depression and anxiety that had plagued him the first year dissolved. His spirit was lifted by his determination and renewed ambition.

The man of the house strived to remain useful at home, and the kitchen was his favorite place to take charge. Stalebread found comfort in the kitchen, with its orderly layout, everything within reach or just a few steps away, and everything just where it belonged. "A place for everything, and everything in its place" was his favorite saying. And he found chopping vegetables, peeling potatoes, and washing dishes therapeutic.

One welcome addition to the family came as a surprise in 1901. Olga purchased a beautiful Steinway upright piano from the Grunewald Music Store on Canal Street. Olga had the piano delivered to the Lacoumes' residence on Christmas Day. Within a year, Stalebread was singing and accompanying himself proficiently on the piano, telling everyone that someday he would become a Professor. The piano sat under the wall-mounted telephone, and he played for Olga from his latest compositions whenever she called.

Out of the darkness emerged a resolute musician ready to resume his career. His Steinway piano provided another level of professional challenge; he rose to the challenge by practicing for hours every day.

16. The Return

The cat came back, it just wouldn't stay away...

THE RAZZY DAZZY SPASM BAND'S SUDDEN disappearance in 1900 triggered speculation on the streets at first, but the sad reason behind their absence soon became known. The Razzy Dazzy Spasm Band had been the most recognizable band in New Orleans, but no one would have recognized them three years later. After disappearing from the limelight, each of the bandmembers had begun dressing like the young men they were becoming. Socks and shoes replaced bare feet, trousers replaced knee pants, and they now topped themselves with swanky hats instead of greasy, ink-smeared newsboy caps.

During their disappearance, the bandmembers chose to pursue other incomes, and in the process, each bequeathed their newspaper camps to their young orphan substitutes. Immediately after his tragedy, Stalebread gave up his newspaper camp on Canal and Royal to his trusty six-year-old substitute, Whiskey, because Stalebread's little brother Jimmy was in school.

It also had come time for those at the Newsboys' Home to relinquish their bunks. Like Jack Dup and all of the other newsboys before them, Warm Gravy, Chinee, Family Haircut, Cajun, Monk, and Stalebread were moving into adult professions. Only Stalebread would continue as a professional musician.

Monk and his brother Cajun opened the Lickety Split Shoe Repair shop downtown, and the carpenter Chris Nielsen helped them construct an eight- by-twelve-foot shack with a walk-up counter for shoe drop-off and pick-up. Nielsen cut out an arched hole at the base of the counter, so people could get an on-the-spot shoeshine for a penny while standing at the counter. Above the hole, Monk hand-lettered a sign: "FAMOUS PENNY LICKETY SPLIT SHINE."

Inside the establishment was a cobbler's bench, flanked by shelves stacked with shoes. The electricity needed to power the lights, lathe, polisher and grinder was legally tapped from the building next door. The only thing they lacked was plumbing. A ladder in the back went up to the cramped loft where there was a cotton mattress and a chamber pot. Installing a retractable glass skylight was Nielsen's idea after he salvaged one from a demolished building. The skylight spanned half of the roof, and served for ventilation and much-needed daylight. With the street-lamp near the shack, it helped at night, too. The Lickety Split business was the brothers' pride and joy.

As a teenager, Warm Gravy became a police informant, or "stool pigeon," as Tom Anderson teased. Warm Gravy started using his real name: Harry Gregson. He had sharp eyes and joked that he could see around corners. He was never caught flat-footed, and claimed he could trail a suspect all day without getting the slip. Most tips he gave to the beat police resulted in arrests. For his efforts, Harry received a weekly stipend of ten dollars. It was much less than the money he made in The Razzy Dazzy Spasm Band's glory days, but the work got his foot in the door at the police department. His mentor, one-time Head of the Detectives Tom Anderson, championed seventeen-year-old Harry in a glowing letter of recommendation, garnering him a full-time salaried position in the detective department.

Family Haircut worked full-time at his family's Tip Top Barbershop, as he always knew he would. He was proud to continue the family tradition. At the barber shop, combs stood in beakers full of blue disinfectant, but Family Haircut's old musical comb always stayed in his shirt pocket to remind him of his days with The Razzy Dazzy Spasm Band. So did the framed studio portrait of the boys that hung on the wall.

When Tom Anderson hired Chinee as a barback at Arlington Annex, Chinee moved out of the Newsboys' Home and rented a room at a boarding house on Rampart Street. He gave his newspaper camp to Booze Bottle, who lived at the Home. Chinee's first job at Tom's saloon was filling the two-quart buckets of beer known as growlers. These were for delivery boys who came and went with the growlers to satisfy thirsty customers elsewhere. While he was filling growlers, he was constantly washing mugs and glasses, bouncing between tasks. Chinee liked his steady job and was making a decent living. Often he looked out the front window, wistfully remembering playing there on the boardwalk with his bandmates.

The subject of a Razzy Dazzy Spasm Band comeback was the most frequently asked question the band members fielded from old friends, fans, and family members alike. Everyone felt the band's disappearance had left a void in New Orleans' music scene. Boys still made homemade instruments, but no spasm bands had formed since Stalebread's band went into hiatus. The Razzy Dazzy Spasm Band members began wondering if spasm was just a one-off that began and ended with their band. Was it only the novelty of their street urchin personas and their homemade instruments that people remembered? Could it live on, or was their invention of spasm obsolete?

When discussing the band's comeback, Stalebread, Warm Gravy, Chinee, Family Haircut, Cajun, and Monk agreed that they wanted spasm to at least return for one last time, for old time's sake.

"Everybody will be scratching their heads when we show up! They won't even recognize us!" the chuckling bandleader speculated. They were all grown up and swanky and wondered, with good reason, if they would be accepted or rejected for their new personas. Stalebread didn't say where and when their eminent comeback might take place, so the band members had to wait for their leader's decision patiently, as they always had done.

In late 1902, fate prompted their comeback.

One block into the French Quarter, Iberville Street ran parallel to Canal Street. Jack Robinson's Haymarket Café stood on the northwest corner of Iberville and Burgundy Street. It was not so much a café as it was a saloon with cold oysters and hot chowder. Jack's place catered to private stag parties, business luncheons, and other reservation-only events. The Haymarket Café had red and white gingham tablecloths, and silverware wrapped in red napkins, which elevated it above the common spittoon saloon.

A young drummer named Johnny Stein, who frequented the Haymarket Café, approached Jack Robinson one day about the possibility of booking monthly stag parties for The Young Businessmen's Association, of which he was a member. Jack's eyes lit up when Stein promised the Haymarket Café would be packed whenever the YBA held an event. He was told their membership was nearly 100.

Johnny had recently formed a small band of other musicians from the Young Businessmen's Association who wanted to be in a hot band. He recruited Gus Shindler on piano, guitar, and cornet; Yellow Nunez on clarinet; Harry Huguenot on bass fiddle; Frank Christian on guitar; and Johnny played drums. New Orleans was now home to a few up-and-coming hot bands. Johnny's band intended to play at the association's monthly stag parties, when they found a place big enough to hold them.

Jack was particularly happy to hear this, because the Haymarket had a capacity of 100. Jack showed Johnny where the stage would be set for them when they played at his place. "By the way, if you fellas are any good, maybe you could be my house band," Jack teased, adding, "I guarantee the success of the band who goes along with the idea I have."

Johnny was all ears as Jack introduced his idea by asking him if he remembered The Razzy Dazzy Spasm Band. "Oh yeah!" he answered.

"Well, Johnny, when was the last time you heard them?"

Johnny thought for a moment. "I don't know, I seen them a couple of years ago, maybe, I guess. Maybe more. Why?"

Jack unfolded a piece of paper and showed Johnny The Razzy Dazzy Spasm Band's old set list, handwritten in pencil. As Johnny read the list of songs, Jack continued his pitch: "My cook, Oscar, was a big fan of theirs. Yeah, me and Oscar were talking, and he told me he remembered all their songs. That got me thinking, so I asked him to write down all of their songs he could remember. You know these songs?" he inquired, pointing at his list.

"Well, sure. I bet I know most of them, well enough to whistle, anyway. Why?"

Jack continued, "See, I'm looking for a band that can play these songs hot without reading sheet music to do 'em. Like The Razzy Dazzy Spasm Band used to do 'em. Can your band do 'em without sheet music?"

"Our band has only had two practice sessions." Johnny replied, "but I suppose we could wing it if we tried. We've talked about trying that."

Leaning in, Jack asked, "Can you play hot?"

"That's what my band is doing. That's what we're doing."

Jack shook his head agreeably, "Fine, fine. I'm glad to

hear that. See, I got to thinkin', The Razzy Dazzy Spasm Band, they had it all going on, with their herky-jerky spasm dancing, their beats, their hollers, all that wild stuff they used to do. Do you remember those hollers of Stalebread's? 'Hi Dee Hi Dee Hidee Hi,' and '*Hot* cha cha cha cha.' Do you remember them? That stuff was great, wasn't it? Suddenly they just up and quit, *poof!* Disappeared, and all of that good stuff went to waste. It's a downright shame." Jack snapped his fingers. "*Poof,* gone just like that! I started thinking, why should all that good stuff go to waste?"

Johnny was becoming agitated as he asked, "What are you getting at, Jack?"

Jack cut to the chase, leaning in even closer. "I'm wanting a hot band to learn The Razzy Dazzy Spasm Band's set list, and rag 'em the way they used to do. Hopefully, throw in some of their antics for good measure, too. The shouts and stuff—you know."

"That's it?" Johnny was suspicious of Jack's intentions.

"Well, yeah, more or less. I mean, I don't expect you to show up in bare feet and knee pants."

Johnny probed further. "So you want us to play these songs and just imitate them? My guys are too old for any of that kid's stuff. We all play real instruments, Jack. I just bought an expensive Rogers drum kit, you know. We wouldn't sound much like them—I can tell you right now."

"Now, wait a minute, Johnny, don't be silly. I just want you to play those songs *like* them, but your band will be more sophisticated sounding. Trust me. Hell, no one could sound as primitive as they did. Besides, I'm counting on your *professionalism* as an improvement, see?"

Once again, Johnny pushed back, "So, let me get this straight: We just have to play these songs, and rag them? As long as you're good with just that, I'm good with just that."

Jack smiled, and said, "Well, if you throw in some of the Razzy Dazzy shouts, that would be good, too."

Johnny conceded, "I suppose we can pepper it up with Stalebread's '*Hot* cha cha chas' and 'Hidee hidee hos,' but no dancing around while we're playing? We can't pull off those monkeyshines and play at the same time, like they did. They could do it all and do it all at once."

Jack offered his hand to Johnny, "That's good enough for me, Johnny."

Johnny reluctantly shook Jack's hand and sealed the deal. They agreed the stag parties would be held at The Haymarket Café on the last Friday of each month. At the YBA's next meeting the following evening, Johnny confirmed he had secured a place for their stag parties.

Stein explained to his band the deal he made with Jack, justifying The Razzy Dazzy aspect—playing their songs without sheet music. "It's just a gimmick Robinson came up with. We wanted to try playin' without reading, so here's our chance! Might as well start raggin' with this old list. Some great songs on the list." To his relief, Stein's bandmates liked the challenge of winging it without sheet music, and they were fine with the set list. This made Johnny feel better about his Faustian bargain with Jack Robinson.

One of Johnny's musicians was Yellow Nunez, a

guitarist who had recently taken up the clarinet. This would be his first gig with his new instrument. Nunez owned a mule-drawn drayage wagon and made his living hauling furniture and other loads. Around dusk on the day of the first Haymarket YBA stag party, Nunez pulled his wagon, loaded with bandmembers and their instruments, into the alley behind Robinson's club, and parked next to the back door. The musicians jumped off with their instruments. Jack Robinson was there to greet them in the alley and he helped Johnny unload his drums and carry them inside. Jack had set up their stage just as promised. It was eight by ten feet, and two feet high, festooned with red, white, and blue bunting, with a string of white lights at the border. Their host pointed toward the swinging barroom doors, saying, "It's the best spot in the house—right across from the entrance. They'll hear you three blocks away, Johnny!"

After arranging their instruments on the stage, the musicians bellied up to the bar, where Jack had frosty mugs of beer and shot glasses of whiskey waiting for them.

"Compliments of the house," he proclaimed, raising his shot glass for a toast. "Drinks are on the house for the band, all night." While they drank, Johnny noticed the back of a cloth banner hanging in the front window. The sunlight passed through the banner, revealing the writing on the other side. Out of curiosity, Johnny strolled outside, beer in hand, to see what the banner said, and to his surprise, it was announcing tonight's show as "The Razzy Dazzy Spasm Band."

Johnny came back in, now hot under the collar, and confronted the club owner in front of the band. "What on earth are you trying to do, Jack? We never agreed to use their *name!*" Anyway, this is a private party. You didn't need to advertise! What the hell?"

"What's the problem, Johnny?" Jack asked.

"What's the problem?" Johnny growled back in Jack's face, pointing to the sign hanging outside the window.

Jack was dismissive. "Oh, that. I'm just trying out the name. If you don't fit the bill, I'll find another band that will."

The other band members filed out the front door to see what the issue was, and they all returned, siding with Johnny.

Jack tried to cajole them all. "Come on, fellas, it's just a name, and you don't even have a name yet. You have to admit that it *is* a great band name and it's been going to waste. Besides, it doesn't say 'The Return of' or 'Reunion of,' or anything like that."

Johnny shot back, "It's false advertising, Jack."

Jack held his ground, defiant, and his tone became unpleasant. "Use it or I'll find another band who will. For tonight, I'm introducing you as The Razzy Dazzy Spasm Band. Otherwise, you can pack up right now and go home."

Johnny and his band members huddled at the bandstand to discuss their dilemma. They headed back to the bar, and reluctantly accepted Jack's offer.

Johnny spoke up for the band. "You had no business doing that, Jack. We don't like what you did one damned bit, but we want to play tonight. We have our crowd showing up in a little while."

Jack grinned and eagerly refilled their shot glasses. "All right, then. Let's drink to that," he concluded.

Even after their second whiskey, the band members were still disturbed by Jack's chicanery, but they soon simmered down and got back to setting up.

Johnny arranged his drum kit while the others tuned their instruments and polished their brass. Within the hour, members of the Young Businessmen's Association and their guests began arriving. Just as Johnny promised, the Haymarket Café was filling up with the Association's dapper young businessmen.

About this time, Stalebread's eleven-year-old brother Jimmy passed the Haymarket Café with his friends Seven Colors and Whiskey. When Jimmy saw the banner in Jack's window, he stopped dead in his tracks. Jimmy and his companions immediately knew it was fraud. Livid, Jimmy ran home, with Seven Colors and Whiskey racing down Burgundy Street just behind him.

When the three arrived at the Lacoumes' street level apartment on Bienville, Stalebread was on the front stoop playing his banjo. "What's up, Blameless?" Stalebread asked, recognizing the sound of his little brother panting. Seven Colors and Whiskey caught up.

"Who's that with you?"

Seven Colors and Whiskey answered for themselves, while Jimmy caught his breath and thought of how to put it to his brother. "Someone stole your band name."

Stalebread tilted his head and stoically contemplated what he was hearing about the banner in the window. After a short pause, he instructed his little brother, "Go in and call my boys. Their numbers are on the telephone table. Tell them to get over here, pronto, and bring their instruments."

Jimmy went inside to make rapid-fire phone calls. Seven Colors and Whiskey stayed with Stalebread, who had resumed playing his banjo as if nothing had happened. He asked them if they recognized the song he was playing, but neither of them did. "This is by Louis Gottschalk," he informed his audience of two. "It's called 'The Banjo.'"

Stalebread's clarion call had gone out to Chinee, Warm Gravy, Cajun, Monk, and Family Haircut. Each of them stopped what they were doing, grabbed their instruments and hot-footed it over to the Lacoumes' place. Word was already getting out on the street about the Haymarket Café banner, and more French Quarter kids headed to 935 Bienville.

Stalebread's old bandmates arrived to find him singing and playing banjo with an audience of a dozen or so neighborhood kids. Everyone was singing, "There'll Be a Hot Time in the Old Town Tonight." Next door to the Lacoumes' was the firehouse, Engine No. 7. The Chief and his firemen came out to see what the commotion was all about and stayed for the sing-along. Kids were coming from both ends of Bienville Street and swarmed in front of 935 until the pack had swelled to a couple dozen. When Stalebread's original bandmates were finally assembling, they gathered around him, joining in on an extended version of the popular song, "Won't You Come Home Bill Bailey?"

When the Fire Chief sauntered over to the stoop, he

asked his next-door neighbor, "What's the special occasion, Stalebread?"

"On the warpath, Chief, I'm sending out a smoke signal," he proclaimed, keeping up with the band's brisk 4/4 beat.

Standing tall on the stoop, Stalebread cupped his hands around his mouth and amplified his old call-and-response "Hidee hidee hidee hi!" He cupped his hands behind his ears next, signaling for their response. The crowd hollered back in unison, "Hidee hidee hidee ho!" He called out the second part of the stanza, "Hodee hodee hodee ho!" and the crowd responded in kind. Even the firemen chimed in. This was chanted over and over until he'd whipped everyone into a frenzy.

Stalebread gathered his bandmates into a huddle. Warm Gravy, Family Haircut, Cajun, Monk, and Chinee draped their arms around each other, and Stalebread grinned sardonically, telling them, "Well, boys, we finally got our big comeback's where and when settled. But first, we've got some business to take care of. Some sons of bitches stole our name!"

Stalebread slung his banjo across his shoulder and put one arm on Jimmy, saying, "Okay, Blameless, take me to the Haymarket Café!" With that he gave the high sign and the crowd made way for the band's passage. Stalebread's entourage passed through the crowd, which in turn fell in behind them. Their number increased steadily along the way. The herd went up Bienville, turning left at Burgundy Street. They marched in legion down Burgundy toward the Haymarket Café. At their leader's command, bandmembers picked up rocks, bricks, and bottles, as they marched. By the time the mob reached Iberville Street, the band members carried ordnance in each hand. The majority of the entourage behind the band remained unarmed.

Blameless stopped the parade at the corner of Iberville and Burgundy, cater-corner to the Haymarket Café. "Halt!" he barked loudly, acting as his big brother's sergeant-at-arms. Jack Robinson's banner was still hanging in the window and everyone read it aloud. "We're here," Jimmy informed his big brother.

"The Haymarket Café is right across the street there, right?" Stalebread reckoned.

"Yep. Dead ahead." Blameless put a rock in his brother's free hand. Stalebread was now armed and dangerous, just like the rest of his boys.

"Hang on tight, little brother," Stalebread said.

Keeping a firm grip on Jimmy's shoulder, he stepped off the curb, and the bandmembers joined the Lacoume brothers, crossing the intersection diagonally toward the Haymarket Café. The rest of the mob stayed put. As the group of seven got closer to the Haymarket's front porch, they heard the old standard, "Rosie O'Grady," coming from inside. The Razzy Dazzy Spasm Band arrived together on the sidewalk in front of the Haymarket Café, pausing to listen to these pretenders for a moment.

"They're not half bad," Stalebread said. He paused and feigned sympathy for them, adding, "Too bad."

Cajun and Monk pushed the swinging saloon doors and the real Razzy Dazzy Spasm Band stood together in the threshold, all six of them plus Jimmy. Stalebread was in the center of the gang, with Jimmy as his right-hand man.

At first, neither Stein's band nor anyone else inside seemed to notice the interlopers. They had just started playing "The Cat Came Back."

The cat had come back, indeed. "JACK ROBINSON!" Stalebread yelled. The whole room fell quiet, save for a few whispers.

Jack was setting up drinks, and when he heard his name called out, he instinctively dropped behind the bar and hid.

Once Stalebread had everyone's attention, he announced to all, "The REAL Razzy Dazzy Spasm Band come here to take our name back!" He turned to his gang and gave the order, "Let 'em have it, boys!"

With that, the band members launched their first salvo. Partygoers and staff dove for cover under tables. Stein's band members ducked and tried to shield themselves and their instruments from the volley of flying projectiles. A brick tore a hole in the skin of Johnny's bass drum. A rock gashed Frank Christian's right knee. Yellow Nunez dodged one chunk of concrete, but a bottle knocked his derby hat off his head. Luckily for him, Yellow's new clarinet went unscathed. The bass player Harry Huguenot dropped down onto the stage and he and his double fiddle took no direct hits. A second barrage followed immediately. Before their ammunition was spent, not a person was left standing in the Haymarket besides the young avengers.

Stalebread put his hand back on Jimmy's shoulder and

said, "Come on, Blameless, let's go home. This party is dead."

With that order, Jimmy turned his brother around and led him back outside. The boys applauded Warm Gravy as he removed the banner and stuffed it into the trash can. The crowd across the street cheered when Stalebread and company reemerged and came marching back across the street. Stalebread, Blameless, Warm Gravy, Chinee, Family Haircut, Cajun, and Monk stopped in the middle of the intersection to simultaneously bellow, "Hurrah!"

Rejoining the jubilance outside, the boys and their second line triumphantly paraded back down Burgundy to 935 Bienville Street. Outside the Lacoume residence, the block party resumed. The firemen occasionally blared their siren, and rang the firetruck's bell in celebration.

"We're back!" hollered Stalebread. "The Razzy Dazzy Spasm Band is BACK!" The crowd cheered. The one-and-only Razzy Dazzy Spasm Band broke into their rendition of "The Cat Came Back." They played the old-time reel, "Mississippi Sawyer," and, reaching back into their old repertoire, they reclaimed "Rosie O'Grady." Jennie and Emma stood in the threshold of their front door and sang along. Jennie played her English concertina. Neighbors came out of their apartments and kids from all over were still streaming in. There must have been sixty partiers on this block of Bienville Street for the Razzy Dazzy Spasm Band's bona-fide comeback concert. Their reunion had finally come about, but no one could have predicted such a wild one.

French Quarter kids would talk about this day for years to come, with many of them swearing they were there that day, even though they hadn't been. No police were called to the Haymarket Café and none were called to break up the street party. Everyone assumed this was divine intervention.

Stalebread and Johnny Stein would cross paths many times in the years to come, and they had some good laughs over each other's accounts of that legendary incident. Neither held a grudge. They both blamed Jack Robinson's chicanery. According to Stalebread's widow, Annie, even Stalebread and Jack Robinson later became friends.

17. THOSE DOUBLE ZS

Hot *cha cha cha cha!*

JOHNNY STEIN AND HIS MUSICIANS DID NOT WANT TO give up on their new band even after the humiliating attack they had just suffered. They all liked how their more sophisticated take on spasm sounded to them and also how well it was being received. They agreed that the Razzy Dazzy Spasm Band's old repertoire came across as their own, just as Jack predicted it would.

Jack Robinson was convinced Johnny Stein's band would do well as his house band, and after the incident, he promised a name change immediately. Johnny warned the proprietor, "They'll want their double Zs back, Jack! Don't say I didn't warn you!"

When Johnny's band returned to play the next evening, they found that, as promised, Jack had had a new banner made. The banner read: "THE RAZZY DAZZY JAZZY BAND." Again, the bandmates were not amused. The name was still, in their view, misleading. Jack had taken the term "jass" and swapped the double Ss for double Zs, to go with "Razzy Dazzy." Jack considered the double Zs fair game. The bandmembers protested, and Johnny argued, "Even this one is libelous, especially now that the real Razzy Dazzy Spasm Band showed up."

Johnny's band played under Jack's new banner for only one night—just long enough to prove themselves invaluable. That second night's performance, billed as "The Razzy Dazzy Jazzy Band," had everyone fearing further revenge, but Stalebread and his mob never returned. Jack Robinson came up with the word "jazzy" to go with his second Razzy Dazzy deceit, and that is the first time those snazzy double Zs replaced the double Ss in "jass." Jack Robinson deserves credit for inventing the spelling of what we now know as jazz.

By the third evening, the band had taken matters into their own hands and came in with a fresh, professionally-made replacement banner of their choosing, heralding their new name: "THE RIGHT AT 'EM RAZZ BAND." Apparently, Johnny and his boys couldn't resist the double Zs, either. Johnny Stein and his bandmates now played the Haymarket Café once a week on Saturdays, and once a month played at the Young Businessmen's Association's stag parties. They would continue to do so for some time. The Right At 'Em Razz Band also entertained a variety of other groups, even getting work in the advertisement business, with, "ballyhoos" playing from the back of Yellow's drayage wagon. The band ballyhooed everything from prize fights to cosmetics; whatever the advertising agent brought them banners for, they'd do it. Ballyhoos were lucrative gigs, especially for Yellow, who owned the wagon.

His take was a full 30 percent for using his wagon, and the rest of the band split the remaining 70 percent. Yellow painted the wagon to match his name, and draped the tailgate with a red oilcloth banner advertising the band: The Right At 'Em Razz Band For Hire! Telephone 1652. The ad man provided banners for each side of the wagon. They made a good name for themselves as The Right At 'Em Razz Band.

In 1915, Johnny Stein assembled another band with two of his Right At 'Em Razz Band alumni, clarinetist Yellow Nunez and cornetist Frank Christian. He called it "Stein's Dixieland Band," and included future greats Henry Ragas on piano and Eddie "Daddy" Edwards on trombone. A Chicago promoter booked them at Schiller's Cafe in Chicago. Christian decided to stay in New Orleans, so Stein hired New Orleans native Dominic James "Nick" LaRocca to replace Frank on cornet. Stein's Dixieland Band went to Chicago and became an overnight sensation.

This roster was short-lived, however, due to the band's immediate success. In 1916, Stein's Dixieland Band broke up. Their success led to getting more lucrative offers to perform elsewhere in Chicago. Stein's name was on the Schiller Café's contract, so he was stuck, but his bandmates were not legally bound and knew they would do better if they started their own band. It must have been difficult informing their boss that he was being replaced by another drummer. They assured Johnny that it was nothing personal. In June, the spinoff band called up Tony "Spargo" Sbarbaro from New Orleans to replace their old bandleader on drums. Johnny assured them he understood, and hired replacement bandmembers so he could fulfill his contract.

Everyone in the spinoff Dixieland band at this time was a veteran of "Papa Jack" Laine's Reliance Brass Band. LaRocca assumed leadership and they named themselves The Original Dixieland Jass Band. Within the year, they changed out the double Ss in their name for those irresistible double Zs. They recorded once under the name The Original Dixieland Ja<u>ss</u> Band for The Victor Talking Machine Company. In February of 1917, the band recorded many standards, but their novelty song "Livery Stable Blues" from those sessions was the first jazz song ever issued on a physical record. The song's hook was the hokum barnyard imitations Johnny had cribbed from The Razzy Dazzy Spasm Band, who had originally cribbed them from Doc Mulney's Minstrel Show and other minstrel shows. "Livery Stable Blues" was also the first hit jazz record in history. Nick LaRocca penned their next huge hit late in 1917. By then they had permanently changed the spelling and the double Zs would forevermore be the way "jazz" was spelled.

Not long after The Original Dixieland Jazz Band's hit exploded, Nick LaRocca was quoted in newspapers claiming to have invented jazz. This claim would become rather common; besides LaRocca (born in 1889), Freddie Keppard (born in 1889), Jelly Roll Morton (born in 1890), George Vetiala "Papa Jack" Laine (born in 1873), and Stalebread Lacoume (born in 1885) all claimed to have invented the music genre. Some of the youngest pretenders even changed their date of birth for the sake of plausibility. Stalebread made the claim that he started out on his own in 1893, which was accurate, but Papa Jack Laine cited his own timeline; Jack was already twelve when Stalebread was born. Many claimed the title without challenge or animosity. All musicians appreciated the need for self-promotion. No one gave much thought to this until jazz history became a scholarly subject in the 1930s. Academics would characterize these competing claims as controversial.

In 1946, after Stalebread's passing, his widow Annie included the inscription on the Lacoume family's tombstone: "EMILE STALEBREAD LACOUME, ORIGINATOR OF JAZZ MUSIC." This inscription has rankled the ire of some academics.

Lacoume family headstone, St. Patrick's Cemetery in Metairie

Johnny Stein continued to do well as a bandleader, despite being marooned in Chicago by his old bandmembers. In 1918, Johnny attended an Original Dixieland Jazz Band concert in New York City. At the concert, he met vaudeville legend James Francis "Jimmy The Snozola" Durante. The vaudeville star Jimmy Durante had played jazz piano from an early age. He dropped out of seventh grade to play ragtime piano professionally. Jimmy wanted his own jazz band, so when he met Johnny Stein, he offered him the job as his bandleader, and Stein took it. Stein was put in charge of recruiting for Durante's band, and naturally brought in more of Papa Jack's alumni, including clarinetist Achille Baquet.

When frontman, pianist, singer, comedian and all-around vaudeville entertainer Jimmy Durante called his new band "Durante's Jazz and Novelty Band," he too adopted those irresistible double Zs. Jimmy was also the beneficiary of Stein's old bag of tricks that reached back to The Razzy Dazzy Spasm Band and his Right At 'Em Razz Band. A consummate comedian, Jimmy loved the old gimmicks Stein brought with him. "*Hot* cha cha cha cha" so enthralled him that he immediately made it his own. This catchphrase became Durante's signature exclamation for the rest of his life.

18. ALL GROWN UP

They expect you to be the same as the last time they seen you,
not all dressed up and swanky.

By 1903, STALEBREAD WAS NO LONGER PLAYING EVERY
day with the Razzy Dazzy Spasm Band. He was mostly
earning his living as a solo entertainer accompanying
himself on piano, guitar and banjo for private parties. Of
the six original band members, he was the only one still
making his living as a musician. The others were busy with
their own careers and only found time to get together once
or twice a week, at best, and more for the camaraderie
than for the money.

In the District, no one cared that they were now
dressing in finery. The band was grateful not to be judged
in the District for having grown up and changed their
appearance, and Tom Anderson still welcomed them with
genuine hospitality.

This was not the case with some promoters, however.

Doc Mulney, for one, had no use for their new "mature" image, and stopped hiring them after their comeback. This did not upset the band, as it was just Doc Mulney's hackneyed old minstrel show anyway. Doc complained, "You lost your look. Y'all dress better than me now." He was trying his best to explain, "People expect to see those barefoot newsboys when they come see The Razzy Dazzy Spasm Band. They expect you to be the same as the last time they seen you—not all dressed up and swanky."

"I never ask any act to even 'cork-up' for my oleo, but jeeze, Louise, it's an oleo in a minstrel show, fer Christ sakes. Everyone's got to look silly somehow. My audiences don't want to see no sharp-dressed spasm band. My audiences want to see acts that are on the lower end of the totem pole than they are, see? They need someone lowlier than them to laugh at. Your street urchin get-up always fit the bill perfectly, but now, y'all ruined your act. You're too swanky now. If I put y'all out there like this, y'all will make my audiences uncomfortable. See my point?" The boys understood Doc's logic, and both parties cordially ended their long professional association.

Outside the District, their little park across the street from the Tulane and Crescent theaters felt like home. They dressed as nicely as they pleased and no one questioned them about their metamorphosis. They were as polite as they always had been, which made them even more endearing as prodigal sons reappearing after their long hiatus. At the park, old friends dropped by to hang out, and those friends often brought new ones to meet the band. Chaperoned young ladies also stopped by to book the dapper young band for soirees and sorority events in the Garden District.

The band's stomping ground outside the Crescent and Tulane theaters

They were playing in their park one day in the fall of 1903 when, out of the blue, an old friend stopped by, the now-world-famous actor William Farnum, from their Canal Street days. He happened to be on his way to the Tulane Theater, where he was performing that night. The boys had first met him in front of The Grand Opera House on Canal Street, when Farnum was the leading man in a stock company years earlier. "Bill" Farnum was also friends with Olga Nethersole and Stalebread knew they were close friends, too. Bill was shocked when he saw that Stalebread was blind. Instead of asking him about that, he explained his presence. "I'm the lead in *Ben Hur* at

The Tulane. We're in town for a two-week run." Bill gave the band members six complimentary tickets for the Saturday matinee of *Ben Hur*. The guys were thrilled about the free tickets. Knowing the story of how they had met Olga, Bill jokingly insisted, "But don't bring a bouquet, okay!"

William Farnum, star of stage and screen

Toward the end of the show's run, Bill stopped by the park and again found the band playing. He wanted to see how they liked the play. They could not thank him enough.

"It did very well in St. Louis," Bill told them. In fact, *Ben Hur* broke box office records in every city it toured.

Traveling world-class productions showcased international stars, and New Orleans was by far the most supportive city in the South. Stalwart theater producers Klaw and Erlanger had never mounted anything as spectacular as *Ben Hur.* Bill described how the company traveled the country with three special trains and a retinue of 350 people, and every stage where they performed the production had to hold thirty tons. He answered their questions about the spectacular chariot scene, which was everyone's favorite. Bill explained the racetrack's engineering, "Did you notice the treadmill the horses gallop on? Well, the treadmill powers the revolving backdrop and makes the chariot's wheels spin!"

"What about those cables attached to the horses' harnesses?" one of the boys asked.

"That's to keep the horses from bolting off the stage. And the big fans kick up the sawdust on a racetrack—they're horse-powered too. Such a great touch, don't you think?"

Ben Hur was the highlight of the 1903 theater season in New Orleans. After its two-week run at the Tulane, William Farnum and his theater troop had an engagement in Atlanta.

Before leaving town, Bill stopped by the park one last time to say farewell.

"Have you heard from Olga lately?" Bill asked.

"We talk every couple of weeks," Stalebread replied nonchalantly.

"Do give her my love, Stalebread," Bill pined. "It seems we're always on the road at the same time, and never cross paths anymore."

"You vagabond actors never stay put in one place long," Stalebread commiserated. "I'll put in a good word for you next time she calls." The two friends would not see each other again until Bill's return three years later to the Tulane in 1906 for the production of *The Prince of India*.

19. Yellow Fever

1904 was a dark year in New Orleans. The yellow fever epidemic had once again sprung up in the city.

Throughout the nineteenth century, New Orleans had enough Yellow Scourges to earn itself the nickname Necropolis, the "City of the Dead." The worst year was 1878, when 4,046 people died. The National Board of Health and the Auxiliary Sanitary Association had seen the worst of it, and prepared for the next epidemic with extremely strict guidelines regarding isolation and hygiene that had long ago been put on the books in the event of such an emergency. The quarantine of 1904 was a result of that vigilance. No one was allowed to leave the city for two years.

The quarantine affected New Orleans financially, socially, and on every level. For one thing, yellow fever divided the population in two. A person who survived a bout with the disease was inoculated for life, and was deemed "'acclimated." Everyone else were "the unacclimated." This binary split had many social ramifications. The acclimated person's social status was automatically elevated. For instance, the acclimated eligible bachelors and bachelorettes were considered better marriage material. Meanwhile, the unacclimated were discriminated against because of their potential to fall ill with yellow fever. The epidemic caused suspicion on many levels as white supremacists scapegoated immigrants, and most people stayed close to their family members, believing the plague would strike only those other than themselves. Some called it "The Stranger's Disease," which speaks to the superstitions and suspicions people harbored at the time.

Audiences dwindled everywhere within the city, and once-busy bands like The Razzy Dazzy Spasm Band played sporadically. The Tulane and Crescent theaters ordinarily closed every summer due to the oppressive heat, but during the yellow fever of 1904 and 1905, they remained shut through both years. The strict quarantine laws allowed people to come into the city but once people were in the city, they weren't allowed to leave. New Orleans was literally "avoided like the plague." Nationally subsidized theater productions indefinitely postponed their plans to visit New Orleans. The city's theater season of 1904–1905, which would normally have begun in early fall, were cancelled altogether.

Without the linchpin of live entertainment, New Orleans nightlife suffered. People were not out drinking and dining because of the epidemic. Fear of the "yellow scourge" made it difficult to earn a living for hospitality workers, and for those who typically made their money on the streets: newsboys, street vendors, buskers, and everyone else, right down to the pickpockets.

During the New Orleans quarantines, The District also suffered greatly, and would have been a complete ghost town if not for the support of the local sporting gents visiting the brothels regularly. The Razzy Dazzy Spasm Band avoided the District altogether during the quarantines. Four miles outside the city, the parks on the breezy shores of Lake Pontchartrain taunted the residents of New Orleans, who would have flocked to its beaches to escape the stifling heat if not for the quarantine trapping them in their city.

During the quarantine, Stalebread was not earning nearly as much as he had gotten used to. Jennie's income from the French Opera covered their basic family expenses, however, and they lived well. Luckily for them, the French Opera was patronized by locals and did not rely on the tourist trade. Stalebread still earned enough to continue paying his siblings' tuition and began replenishing his savings account, which had been depleted during his two-year hiatus. He also never gave up on his goal to one day be a homeowner, which he eventually achieved. Stalebread always credited Miss Wright's Night School for providing him with the business acumen to accomplish his life goals.

During these years, Stalebread concentrated on his solo piano playing, teaching, and singing. He also played guitar with the singing mandolin player, Sou Sou Oramos. Sou Sou was from a small town called Chalmette, near the site of the Battle of New Orleans, along the Mississippi River at English Turn. The singer and mandolin player was raised in a musical family, and had come up to New Orleans by himself to pursue a music career. He got stuck in the city during the quarantines, which was when he joined up with Stalebread.

Stalebread and Sou Sou played all over town as a duet, to the delight of those lucky enough to hear them. They had become fast friends, having discovered their mutual interest in turning any old song hot. Sou Sou favored heating up folk songs, so when he started mixing it up with Stalebread, the two tapped into the Lacoumes' collection of English broadsides. Stalebread knew most of the English, Irish, Scottish, and old-timey American songs, and they ragged them all. The first tune they worked on together was an old sea-shanty broadside ballad called, "Johnny Boker." Stalebread played guitar, Sou Sou played mandolin and they both sang:

> Oh! Do, my Johnny Boker
> Come rock and roll me over
> Do! My Johnny Boker, do!

Another broadside ballad was the Irish song "The Unfortunate Lad," also known as "The Young Man Cut Down in His Prime," a morality tale about a soldier who spent his money on prostitutes and died of venereal disease. Fast-living and ill-fated men were themes of many of these broadsides, and a sure-fire crowd-pleaser was the "Ballad of Jesse James," in which the protagonist's demise is portrayed as heroic.

Sou Sou's favorite ballad was "Spanish Johnny," about a wicked mandolin player who is hanged by the neck:

> The hand so tender to a child
> Had killed so many men.
> He died a hard death long ago
> Before the road came in.
> The night before he swung
>   he sang
> To his mandolin.

Sou Sou translated the song into Spanish, and when they played it together, Stalebread sang the English lyrics and Sou Sou followed in Spanish.

Stalebread also enjoyed playing "Didn't He Ramble," about another ill-fated wanderer:

> Didn't he ramble?
> Didn't he roam?
> Didn't he wander?
> So far from his home…

As is typical of these broadside ballads, the protagonist soon stumbles into trouble, and Stalebread and Sou Sou sang plaintively:

> And didn't he go down?
> Take it all to the grave
> And don't we fare well now
> With the choice that he made

Their repertoire included drinking songs—but not just happy ones like "Little Brown Jug." They also included the morose "Rye Whiskey":

Rye whiskey, rye whiskey,
You're no friend to me,
You killed my poor daddy,
God damned you, try me.

They often went Uptown to play outside the gates of Audubon Park, and did well working that end of town. Another favorite neighborhood was the Irish Channel, where folks congregated outside the merchants' shops. The duo's songs were familiar ones, old Razzy Dazzy numbers like "The Cat Came Back," "Hot Time in the Old Town Tonight," "Rosie O'Grady," and, of course, "Over the Waves," which Sou Sou sang in Spanish. Sou Sou also sang "La Paloma" in its original tongue. The pair made good tips in the Irish Channel.

Sou Sou would help Stalebread off or onto the curbs with a light touch under his friend's elbow. As people stopped to chat and shake Stalebread's hand, Sou Sou knew he was shepherding a living legend. After losing his sight, Stalebread had developed a talent for recognizing a person by their voice.

In 1905, the twenty-year-old Stalebread was hired to play banjo in George Vetiala "Papa Jack" Laine's Reliance Brass Band. Like the French Opera, brass bands relied on local support to get through the quarantine period. Stalebread's new friends in The Reliance Brass Band were his younger bandmates, brothers Merritt and Abbie Brunies, and Mickie Marcour and Charlie Cordella.

Stalebread Lacoume was a local legend and no one was more excited to be playing with him than Papa Jack's youngest band members. Stalebread could relate to these kids, and they to him. The Razzy Dazzy Spasm Band had been revered for years by the youngest of these musicians. He told them stories of the old days, like when The Razzy Dazzy Band had their day in court and Old Judge Bezou labeled them "Spasm," and some of them had already heard the legendary story of their blitz of the Haymarket Café.

Many youngsters had been inspired to become musicians after seeing Stalebread and his crew perform. Ten-year-old cornetist Merritt Brunies recounted to Stalebread, "My father took us to see The Razzy Dazzy Spasm Band once in the Irish Channel on St. Patrick's Day!" Eventually, Jack Laine's son, Albert, whom everyone called "Baby" Laine or "Patsy," began tagging along with the boys until his father made him an official member of the marching band. Among this bunch of young musicians, Stalebread found a new group of young players to work with, and for the next three decades of their careers. Stalebread played with these future jazz stars in duos, trios, four-piece five-piece, and even big bands.

The most important of these bands was Abbie Brunies' Halfway House Orchestra, (named for being "halfway" between the City and Lake Pontchartrain). Nineteen-year-old Abbie Brunies was the bandleader of the newly formed group in 1919, and he immediately hired his old friend, thirty-four-year-old Stalebread as his banjo player. The Halfway House Orchestra gained international fame in the 1920s when the Okeh label began recording them in New Orleans. This is one of the times when Stalebread may have participated in a recording session, but, as George

Buck concluded from his search, no credits or studio logs verify Stalebread's presence on any Okeh recordings.

The Halfway House Orchestra, Stalebread, center

The Four Jazz Babies: Buck Rogers, bandleader Abbie Brunies, Mickey Marcour, and Stalebread Lacoume

The Brunies' father, a violin teacher, became the patriarch of a jazz dynasty when all of the Brunies siblings became professional jazz musicians.

In 1920 Abbie also led another dance band that played at the Halfway House, the Four Jazz Babies, a band that never recorded: Abbie Brunies on trumpet, Emmitt "Buck" Rogers on drums, Stalebread Lacoume on banjo, guitar, and vocals, and Mickie Marcour on piano. Likewise, during the 1920s, Abbie formed another hot combo that never recorded, a trio formed with the intent of playing outdoors, along the shore of Lake Pontchartrain: Charlie Cordella on clarinet, Abbie Brunies on cornet, and Stalebread on guitar and vocals. The three troubadours called themselves the Lakefront Loungers. They serenaded passersby on the lakefront, and sometimes made it over to the Fair Grounds on race days. The trio dressed casually in open-collared shirts and rolled-up sleeves, their breezy style perfectly suited for the Lakefront scene.

The Lakefront Loungers: Charlie Cordella (left) Abbie Brunies, and Stalebread (right)

PART THREE
MAHOGANY HALL

20. Olga, Sarah, and Bill

Internationally renowned French actress Sarah
Bernhardt

1906 WAS A GREAT YEAR FOR NEW ORLEANS, WITH the yellow fever epidemic behind it, the quarantine lifted, and the city returned to relative normalcy. The theater schedule was announced with fanfare in all the newspapers. Stalebread was thrilled to read that Olga Nethersole would be returning to the Tulane Theater in a production of *Carmen*, to be co-produced by her brother, Louis Nethersole.

Olga had kept in close touch with Stalebread over the years, but she hadn't visited the Crescent City in years. Twenty-one-year-old Stalebread was now an accomplished pianist, thanks to her Christmas present five years earlier. He was looking forward to playing for her in person. Over the phone, Olga always enjoyed hearing him accompany himself on the piano to her favorite song, "The Daring Young Man on the Flying Trapeze." She also looked forward to hearing him in person.

> Once I was happy but now I'm
> forlorn
> Like an old coat that is tatter'd
> and torn
> Left on this wide world to fret and
> to mourn
> Betray'd by a maid in her teens
> The girl I lov'd she was handsome
> I tried all I knew her to please
> But I could not please her one
> quarter so well
> Like that man upon the trapeze

... He'd fly thro' the air with the
    greatest of ease
A daring young man on the flying
    trapeze
His movements were graceful
All girls he could please
And my love he purloin'd away

Stalebread, Olga, and Olga's mentor, the world-famous actress Sarah Bernhardt, were all in New Orleans in the fall of 1906. Sarah traveled there to have her private train outfitted for her upcoming "Texas Farewell Tour." Boxcars were added to transport a rented circus tent and enough benches to fill it. Sarah also timed her stopover in New Orleans to support her friend and protégé Olga Nethersole. Stalebread was already in town. Their itineraries inspired this next yarn.

Al Rose, in his book *Storyville*, recounted a legend about Stalebread and Sarah Bernardt's first meeting. Rose described how, according to a "survivor" he interviewed, the two met by chance one night in Storyville: Stalebread was busking with his band, when the boys played "a sidewalk concert" for Sarah Bernhardt while she was "out slumming" in the District. Stalebread complained that Sarah's tip was a pittance.

That claim just never rang true to me. As I got to know Stalebread's and Sarah's personalities over the course of my research, I doubted that story all the more. For one thing, Sarah was no cheapskate.

Left to my own logic, I propose that the two characters were naturally friendly with each other, because of their close friendships with Olga. It's easily explained with this diagram: Stalebread adored Olga (whom he called his "guardian angel"), Olga adored Sarah (who she considered her mentor), Sarah adored Olga (who was her protegee), and Olga adored Stalebread (the son she never had). In my version of this tale, Stalebread and Sarah became fast friends. Stalebread would have been delighted to meet the Divine Sarah Bernhardt, just like everyone else was. Sarah is still referred to as "The Original Rock Star."

Soon after Stalebread learned of Olga's impending return to New Orleans, she telephoned him.

"Stalebread, did you hear I'll be in New Orleans, for *Carmen*? I'm producing and directing with my brother Louis. Also, Bill Farnum will still be in town, closing his *Prince of India* show. Isn't that exciting! And I'm over the moon, as I just found out from Sarah that she will be in town then, too! Wouldn't that be astronomical if we were all together!"

"Even astrological," Stalebread chuckled.

Olga laughed. "You will have to join us! Bill will be glad to see you, and you will absolutely love Sarah."

The seasoned stage actor Bill Farnum and Olga had often been linked as lovers by the press, which was scandalous, as she was ten years older. Regardless, Olga and Bill shared a loving friendship, and were mutual devotees of the indomitable Sarah Bernhardt.

"We'll have my box seats at The Tulane for Bill's last night, and for my opening on the following night. I have a box reserved for my whole run, so you must bring your family to a performance," Olga insisted.

Stalebread pondered the invitation before answering.

"I'll ask my mom. She may think Jimmy and Emma are too young for *Carmen*. Emma is eighteen but Jimmy is only fifteen." Olga understood.

"Tell her I would love to finally meet her."

Olga confided in Stalebread, "I'm so nervous just thinking about Sarah being in the audience for my opening night. After all, she was the perfect *Carmen* years ago. She created the role. I want to be perfect for her. Now, I'll tell you a secret that I have never told you before: Whenever I get nervous before going onstage, which is often, I just remember your bouquet of red roses on the fishing line and how the audience roared as I chased it across the stage. Somehow that memory always loosens me up and calms me down. You will be at my opening night of *Carmen,* promise me."

"I wouldn't miss it for the world!" he assured her.

Olga adored Sarah, and her professional path followed Sarah's as she starred in the renowned actress' most celebrated roles, including *Sapho*, *Camille*, and *Carmen*.

"I know how much she loves me following in her footsteps. I just hope my *Carmen* pleases her," Olga fretted.

Stalebread insisted, "You'll knock it out of the park!"

Both actresses inspired headlines for their behavior—onstage and off. They were both staunch feminists who supported the suffrage movement in the United States, often at the risk of arrest or deportation. Sexuality and feminism were leading edges of resistance against the restrictive social mores and gender roles of the dying Victorian era. These women pushed boundaries with their high profiles and their business acumen, and with their provocative performances and their risqué wardrobes.

Being constantly covered in the news served their purpose, too. They were savvy celebrities in their day.

Though thirty-year-old William Farnum was half Sarah's age, he claimed she could drink him under the table. The diva was not only legendary for her progressive social positions and eccentric behavior, but she was also a living legend in the acting community for being a consummate professional. Sarah had been a serious actress ever since she was a young girl. In 1854, she was only ten when she met playwright Alexandre Dumas. He recognized her natural ability, and urged her to pursue a life in the theater. Her mother took that advice seriously, and so did the child. At twenty-three, Sarah had become such a versatile performer that she was even called upon to play roles as both genders in *Athalie,* by Jean Racine.

Sarah's bravery onstage led to many physical injuries. Her right leg was once broken, and was irreparably injured again when a stagehand misplaced a cushion she was supposed to land on. She soldiered on in pain for years, gracefully compensating for her limp. At one point she decided to have her right leg amputated at the knee, but put it off for years. News of this possibility caused a world-wide sensation in the press, with one tabloid claiming that Sarah had actually performed the amputation herself.

The "Divine Sarah Bernhardt" was the first true modern celebrity. She used her name and image on products to support her lavish lifestyle, but her true passion was for tearing down the Victorian standards. Sarah was a constant promoter of women's rights. The public showered adoration upon her despite the fact that she did not uphold the prevailing Victorian standard of beauty. For a leading lady, Sarah was unusual not only for her limp, but also for her scrawny frame in an era that favored voluptuous leading ladies. Dumas once remarked about Sarah, "She has the head of a virgin and the body of a broom." This always inspired Olga, who thought of herself as plain.

Beyond her star appeal, Sarah was also a pioneer in the business of theater. Sarah Bernhardt paved the way for women producers. Olga, like Sarah, was no stranger to the challenges of producing as a woman. Earlier in the year, Olga's own production of Clyde Fitch's *Sapho* in New York City was shut down and the theater was charged with "offenses against public decency" and "creating a public nuisance."

Before Sarah's arrival, Olga related to Stalebread some details she had learned about Sarah's plans and entourage. "Sarah's train will be picking up three additional boxcars in New Orleans to carry the circus tent and benches she's renting. She's calling this her 'Texas Farewell Tour,' but she's used that old publicity ploy before."

"Wow," gushed Stalebread, "her own private train."

Olga told him how lavishly Sarah traveled: "Oh, yes, and it pulls eight cars. Her cargo includes 300 pieces of luggage, two maids, a couple of manservants, her masseuse, her secretary, and her cook. Also, Sarah travels with her menagerie. She has two Russian wolfhounds, a tigress, a boa constrictor, and her pet alligator, Ali Gaga."

Stalebread was looking forward to meeting the most famous woman in the world. "Someday I'll tell my children I met Sarah Bernhardt!" he said. Olga replied jokingly, feigning dejection, "Hey, what am I? Chopped liver?"

Stalebread laughed, "I'll tell them you are my guardian angel."

"Ahh," Olga sighed happily, knowing it was true.

The date finally arrived for closing night of *The Prince of India*. Stalebread was excited to attend as Olga's guest. He was instructed to present himself at the side stage door. For this special occasion, he hailed a hansom cab to pick him up from home and deliver him to the Tulane Theater's stage door entrance. When the cab arrived at the Tulane and parked, the cabbie helped Stalebread down and made sure his suit got a few light swipes from his brush. Stalebread tipped the driver generously.

While waiting to be received at the stage door, he reminisced about standing in that very spot when he was a kid, after he and his boys had been thrown out of the theater.

Olga herself opened the stage door. Stalebread didn't know it was her until he caught the scent of her perfume. The six years between their last meeting vanished. Though she had barely aged in appearance since then, he had grown from a boy into a young man.

"My, oh my, the last time I saw you must have been a long, long, long time ago! Your voice changed over the years, so I don't know why I should be so surprised to see you all grown up? Isn't that funny?" she wondered rhetorically.

Stalebread joked, "You look just the same, Olga." They laughed as she linked her arm with his. She kept looking him up and down as they entered the theater, still amazed at his transformation.

Ushering Stalebread slowly through the corridor, Olga

paused at a staircase and paused. "You and I will join Sarah upstairs, in my private box. Bill is there, too. Shall we?" Stalebread smiled, raising his elbow for her to guide him up the stairs.

When the pair entered Olga's private box, Bill and Sarah stood to greet them, and Olga formally introduced Stalebread to Sarah. The legendary actress offered him her petite hand and he kissed it. After their introduction, Bill stepped forward to greet his old friend. "So good to see you Stalebread. It's been three years! I'm glad that you made it tonight. I hope all your loved ones were spared from the yellow scourge."

"Yes," replied Stalebread, "my family came through unscathed, thank God."

"That's so good to hear," Bill said. "I know it made life miserable for everyone."

Stalebread agreed, sighing, "Let's pray that never happens again."

Now that Olga and Stalebread could attend to Sarah, Bill excused himself. "I must run. We go on soon."

"Break a leg!" Sarah exclaimed. Olga and Stalebread echoed the sentiment.

After the play, Bill returned to Olga's box and the four of them went down to the backstage catering room, where the cast party was already underway. Sarah was the focal point in the room, as she was everywhere she went. No one had the nerve to approach her at first, and she kept Stalebread on her arm for companionship. Olga and Bill made their way around the room, schmoozing with the cast, crew, and other guests.

Sarah was down to earth with her fellow thespians and

readily talked shop. Olga brought Sarah and Stalebread to the piano in a corner of the room. "Stalebread, perhaps you can play something for us?" Olga requested. He was delighted to finally perform for her in person after all these years, and began with his hot rendition of "William Tell Overture," which surprised and delighted the party. "I call this one 'Willie Tell,'" he told them. "This next one is dedicated to Olga," Stalebread announced as he broke into "The Daring Young Man on the Flying Trapeze." Everyone in the room sang along to the popular song. He followed with another familiar tune that kept everyone singing, "Bill Bailey, Won't You Please Come Home." After almost an hour, Sarah, Olga, and Bill decided to leave, and whisked Stalebread away with them.

Waiting in the back alley of the Tulane Theater were two single horse drawn hansom cabs. Sarah asked Stalebread, "Will you be coming to Olga's *Carmen* opening tomorrow night?"

He answered unequivocally, "I would not miss it for the world."

"Splendid. I will see you then," she said, putting her hand in his as she had done before. He trembled as much as he did the first time he kissed her hand.

"See you then."

Bill helped Sarah get into his cab, and turned around to say goodnight to Olga and Stalebread.

"I'll get Sarah back to her train. Thank you both for being here for the closing of my run. Olga, it means so much to me. I can't wait for your opening tomorrow night."

Bill grasped Stalebread's hands for a hearty handshake,

after which Olga gave Bill her famous "Nethersole Kiss." Though he couldn't see them, Stalebread could sense what was going on, which prompted him to exclaim, "*Hot* cha cha cha cha!" This broke the spell, and they all laughed, but Bill's knees went weak, and he had to pause for a moment before climbing into the horse-drawn cab.

Stalebread and Olga remained in the alley talking about the first time they met, a fond memory. "Me and my boys were stage-door Johnnies, weren't we? I didn't care, I was determined to meet you."

"Well, that bouquet was good bait and you reeled me in, Stalebread. I was excited to meet you, too. When the doorman got word to me that you boys were out here waiting for me, I rushed right out."

The two dear friends reminisced about their friendship. When Olga yawned, Stalebread suggested they call it a night.

"You'd better be getting some rest. You have a big day tomorrow," he insisted. They both climbed into the back, aided by the cabbie.

"The theater has this cab at my disposal while I'm in town," she explained, "I'm staying at The Roosevelt. Let me have James give you a ride home after he drops me off," she offered. As they settled in, Olga made her introductions.

"Stalebread, this is James, the most handsome hansom cab driver in all New Orleans, and James, this is my dear friend Stalebread Lacoume. Take him wherever he'd like to go."

"Nice to meet you, Mr. Stalebread," James said from his perch.

"Nice to meet you, James," Stalebread replied. James picked up the reins and clicked his tongue loudly to spur on his horse, Daisy. The ride to Olga's hotel would be a short one, as it was just a few blocks away.

From the corner of Common and Baronne, the cab quickly made its way the few blocks to her hotel.

"They have me in a beautiful suite," she told Stalebread as they pulled up to the front entrance of the hotel. "Bill will meet you at the backstage door tomorrow, half an hour before show time. You'll be with Bill and Sarah in my box again, and I hope your family will come, too. There's plenty of room in my box!"

Stalebread promised he would talk to his mother in the morning.

"I'll see you after the show, and we'll all go to the cast party together," Olga promised.

James went to her side of the cab and helped her down. "See you tomorrow," Stalebread called out as she walked away.

21. Tony Jackson

Where the moon shines, dreams are bought and sold.

"Where to, Mr. Stalebread?" James asked after climbing back into his driver's seat. He was reminding Stalebread of Olga's offer, "Just name your destination. If you're a sportin' gent I can take you down the line and wait around if you want. Have you've ever seen anything like those places on Basin Street? They are really something, I hear!"

His passenger chuckled, nodding his head affectionately. "Yes, I have, James."

Stalebread thought he would be going straight home, but this offer got him thinking. "Do you know Tom Anderson's saloon?" Stalebread asked.

James did not hesitate, "Sure, he calls it the Arlington Annex now, but it's the same place."

Stalebread concurred, "Correct. It used to be The Fair Play Saloon. Take me there." James clicked his tongue and Daisy stepped forward.

Professor Tony Jackson

James guided Daisy up Canal Street toward Tom's Saloon. It was a lively time of night in the District when they made a right turn off Canal Street and into the hubbub of Basin Street. As Daisy plodded her way down Basin, James informed Stalebread, "There on the left is the Terminal Saloon and Few Clothes Cabaret. They're both lousy with pickpockets." Stalebread smiled, remembering when he and his boys were hired as guides and had given those Biloxi fraternity boys the same admonition.

Tom Anderson's saloon, originally called the "Fair Play"

The cab continued its slow pace down the line, until the driver pulled up curbside at Tom's place. Tom was standing on the porch when the cab arrived. He stopped the conversation he was engaged in as soon as he saw Stalebread in the back of the cab. He immediately went over to the carriage to greet his old friend.

"Good to see you, Stalebread. It's been a while."

"Good to see you too, Tom," he replied.

"I have this cab at my disposal, so I thought I'd drop by and say hi to you and Chinee. Is he workin' tonight?"

"Oh yeah, he's behind the bar, serving. Chinee is one of my best bartenders now."

"When's his next break?" Stalebread asked.

"In half an hour."

Stalebread replied, "Well, I'll probably shove off, then. But tell him I stopped by, okay?"

Tom had an idea and asked Stalebread to stay put. "I'll be right back—don't leave."

A minute or so later, Tom came back out with Chinee in tow. Chinee was balancing three neat whiskies on a tray. Tom proposed a toast, and took two of the glasses from Chinee, giving one to Stalebread. "To the good life, and to our good lives. What a helluva wild ride, eh?" Tom waxed. Stalebread and Chinee chimed in with their old, "Hurrah!" The three friends raised their glasses, clinked them together, and drank their whiskey. They talked alongside Stalebread's cab for a while.

"Business good, boys?" asked Stalebread.

Tom answered, "Oh, hell, yeah. The District is booming again, ever since the quarantine ended. Our doors never close, just like old times."

Chinee told his old bandleader, "Hot bands have been coming into the District ever since the quarantine ended, too. I think there's one playing about every night now. Remember when we were the only hot band playing in the District? Boy, we made a lot of dough out on this banquette right here, didn't we? Those were the days, Stalebread."

Stalebread agreed wistfully, "We sure did make some loot back then, we sure did. Yep, those were the days, Chinee."

"You boys were great," Tom added. "These new bands coming into the District, I never hire any of 'em, but they get brought in to play for private stag parties. For regular music, I tell ya, I still rely on my trusty old pianola. I buy new rolls for variety and I'm on a monthly subscription. I get a new roll every month."

"Listen to that baby in there," said Tom. The three paused for a moment. It was plenty loud from where they stood outside. The music coming from the player piano leapt out from the crowded barroom. Men gathered around the pianola and sang along to lyrics so simple even the drunkest of them couldn't forget them.

> Ta ra ra boom dee ay
> Ta ra ra boom dee ay
> Ta ra ra boom dee ay
> Ta ra ra boom dee ay

"That's the latest player roll from my subscription— just arrived today," boasted Tom. Chinee piped up, "And Tom don't let just anyone sit at his pianola anyway."

"Yeah, even though anyone could keep up with pumping the bellow pedal," Tom admitted. "I don't want no ham-handed drunks sitting down trying to play."

They toasted again with their last drops of whiskey. Chinee collected their empty glasses and mentioned to

Stalebread, "Say, that was a fun birthday party your mother threw for you. Your mother's the best."

Stalebread replied, "She really is."

Chinee mused, "The big twenty-one! Wow, you got old, boy. Who ever thought any of us would make it to the ripe old age of twenty-one?"

Tom added his belated birthday wishes. "Congratulations, you're now a man!" All three laughed at that cliché salutation, and Chinee excused himself and went back inside to work.

Tom asked Stalebread, "What have you been up to lately? I haven't seen you in a long time."

"Well, I'm still making music for a living. Kept busy enough to get by through the quarantine. I stayed out of the District, but I was playin' all over town."

"That's great. Whereabout?"

"Well, Papa Jack kept me working in his Reliance Marching Band during the quarantine," Stalebread answered. "He's always got room in one of his Reliance bands for me and my banjo. Papa Jack kept us booked solid every weekend. I love all the old Sousa 4/4 stuff, but you know Jack—he definitely likes to keep up with the modern tunes, too. We did 'Meet Me in St. Louis,' 'In the Good Old Summertime,' 'Bill Bailey.' You know, the crowds are yelling out for the new stuff. No one's shouting for Sousa."

"Yeah, you know what they say," Tom agreed. "'Sousa is for picnics and politics'—everyone wants Sousa on the Fourth of July."

"I also get the private Garden District parties," Stalebread continued. "I like those. They always have their pianos in tune and the hosts always lay out a good spread. No bandmates, just me, the champagne, and the oysters. You know what I mean?" He patted his tummy, and licked his chops.

Tom chuckled. "Stalebread, I remember when you first came around, you were a scrawny pup. All of your band were scrawny little street urchins. But boy, did you grow up *and* out!"

Stalebread admits, "Well, let's just say, life expands in more than one direction." He added, "I've also been playin' guitar and singin' in a duo with my friend Sou Sou Oramos. He's a mandolin player."

"Any relation to Florenzo Ramos?" Tom asked.

Stalebread answered, "No, he gets asked that a lot. Sou Sou's name starts with O, Oramos. No relation. Sou Sou comes from Chalmette."

Sou Sou Oramos (with mandolin and cigarette) and Stalebread (seated, far right, bowing bass fiddle) with The Razzy Dazzy Spasm Band at a West End picnic in 1906. *From Al Rose Collection.*

The Fischbein-Williams Syncopators at the LaVida Dance Hall, 1923. Stalebread on banjo (far right) next to Florenzo Ramos on saxophone.

"Say, Stalebread," Tom had an epiphany, "speaking of pianos, I heard Tony Jackson is playing tonight at Mahogany Hall. You know, Lulu probably has her parlor windows open." Stalebread knew what that meant. When the parlor windows were open, the Professors' music could be heard loud and clear outside on the sidewalk. Lulu White's Mahogany Hall was just a block away.

"This carriage would give me a mighty nice ringside seat. Thanks for that tip! I'll be checking that out. I hope you heard right!"

Tom reassured him. "Tony's boyfriend Eddie was just here a while ago. He told me that's where Tony is playing tonight. Eddie always knows where Tony's at."

Excited, Stalebread bid Tom farewell. "Appreciate the whiskey, Tom, and thanks for the tip about Tony. And while I'm at it, thank you for all you have done for me and the boys, over the years, in the beginning, and after our return, too. Not everyone wanted us comin' back dressed up swanky. A lot of people expected us to stay newsboys forever, I guess."

Tom returned the tribute. "Hell, The Razzy Dazzy Spasm Band has always been welcome at my place, just as much after your comeback as before. And your original band may have scattered, but it's good to hear you are still playing. It does me good to know it."

Stalebread nodded, saying, "You know, everything changes and everything's got an end to it. Me and my boys had a good run though, didn't we?"

Tom emphatically agreed. "You did. You sure as hell did, my friend."

Oblivious to the old hands trading war stories, James was reading the *Blue Book* to pass the time. He was looking at the pages showing the very street they were on, where the Basin Street mansions began next to Tom's.

"Thanks for the tip about Tony, Tom. We'll go to Mahogany Hall right now and see for ourselves."

Tom said farewell and went back into his saloon where the pianola roll had just come to an end and needed reloading.

"Two thirty-five, James," Stalebread instructed gleefully. James clicked his tongue and Daisy walked down the line to Mahogany Hall. In his mind's eye, Stalebread remembered the mansions between Hilma's and Josie's that were nothing unique—Diana's, next to Norma's, Lizette Smith's next to Minnie White's, and Jessie Brown's, which always had all of the requisite trappings of a fine bordello, but nothing eye-popping. Next door to Jessie Brown's was a different story entirely: Josie's Arlington. The Arlington was always abuzz with activity, thanks to Josie's partnership with Tom. He provided a steady stream of primed sporting gents from his saloon.

"We've just passed The Arlington, and now it's Madame Martha Clark's," announced James.

Stalebread knew they were approaching the main attraction: the fabled Mahogany Hall. Lulu White, the proprietor, was the savviest of all the madams on Basin Street. She had been arrested more than all the other madams combined, which mattered little because she was also the most politically connected. She curried favor with a number of well-placed and powerful men, including the city tax assessor. The public record reveals that her first mansion on Custom House Street in the early 1890s had such a low valuation that the property taxes were next to nothing.

"Frank Toro's place still open down the block?" Stalebread asked. Frank Toro's saloon still had the reputation for being the roughest joint in all of The District.

"Oh, yeah, Terrible Toro's, at the end of the line," James said.

"Yeah, they say there's a reason Toro's is near the cemetery," replied his passenger.

James joked back, "Italian gangsters *and* Italian food, both to die for!"

Next door to Frank Toro's was Countess Willie Piazza's mansion. Countess Willie and Lulu had much in common: both cultured madams, draped in diamond jewelry, and fair-complected. They also employed Professors Tony Jackson and the talented young Jelly Roll Morton. These two Madams were duly respectful of each other, and always cordial, unlike other madams with their feuds and petty jealousies.

"I'm parking us below the bay window," James informed his passenger. The carriage halted at the curb in front of Mahogany Hall.

The glossy black cab shone under the street lamp, and the parlor lights flooded from the bay window. James looked into the parlor from his elevated position and caught sight of the twenty-six year-old entertainer Tony Jackson holding court inside. Stalebread and James could hear Tony at the piano, where two well-dressed men stood nearby, with their arms around girls a third their age.

Tony was playing the lament "Break the News to Mother," a song made popular during the Spanish-American War:

> Just break the news to mother
> She knows how much I love her
> And tell her not to wait for me.

Tony performed "My Wild Irish Rose," which made Stalebread smile. Concluding his set, Tony stood up and walked away from the piano.

When James looked down Basin Street, he saw a silhouette of a man running out of Toro's, his hands on his face. The silhouette crossed Bienville and disappeared into the dark. A minute later, two wobbly patrons stepped out of Toro's, and began walking up Basin toward Mahogany Hall. The pair crossed Bienville, and as they did, a hansom cab lurched into motion, trailing them. It crept up Basin behind the tipsy couple. As the pair of silhouettes drew closer, they could be heard singing "(Won't You Come Home) Bill Bailey." Stalebread's ears pricked up.

Mahogany Hall exterior

"A couple of drunks from Toro's coming our way," James announced to his blind passenger. "Don't you worry, Mr. Stalebread. I'll handle them if need be. I got my trusty little pepper box handy." James pulled the four-barreled derringer out of his coat pocket and cocked it, now at the ready.

As the two wobbly pedestrians drew nearer, their cab followed, coming to a halt when they stopped. The short one was a woman and the tall one was a man, James surmised by their silhouettes. Stalebread was unaware that it was Sarah and Bill coming this way, but the two could see Stalebread in the cab. They came over to their friend. The couple were wearing fedoras and when Sarah removed hers, her curly red hair fell to her shoulders.

"Stalebread!" Sarah exclaimed.

Stalebread immediately recognized her voice.

Bill piped up, "She wanted me to take her slumming in the District before escorting her back to her train. She asked for the most low-down joint, so we ended up at Toro's."

Stalebread chided Bill. "You took her to Toro's?"

Bill swore he'd tried to steer her to Tom's first. "Actually, I had every intention of taking her directly to her train, but she wanted me to take her slumming."

Sarah came to her chaperone's defense: "Bill suggested Tom Anderson's, but when I pressed him on it, he admitted Tom's was the safest saloon in the District, which was not what I was asking for. I asked him which saloon had the worst reputation. He told me Toro's. So, I insisted on Toro's."

Stalebread was still bothered.

"Cat got your tongue, Stalebread?" Sarah teased, and changed the subject. "The bartender at Toro's told us to come to Lulu's and catch Tony Jackson."

Stalebread confirmed. "We heard Tony was playing

here, too, and came right over from Tom's." Stalebread couldn't resist chiding Bill again. "Toro's? I can't believe you took her into Toro's."

"She wanted the most dangerous place. What can I say, Stalebread? It is absolutely impossible to say no to this woman. Besides, it was fairly safe in there tonight. I mean, until those two gangsters got into a knife fight and one got the tip of his nose cut off. But our waiter said neither of them got stabbed. At least nobody ended up on the floor. Just the same, I got us out of there, pronto!"

Sarah giggled, adding, "Both bartenders had to search for the nose tip. It's a good thing it landed behind the bar in the ice bin and stayed clean. The bartender who found it wrapped the tip in a napkin and ice and gave it back to the poor fellow. He just ran out of there with it. I do hope he finds someone to sew it back on for him. I'm sure it's salvageable."

Stalebread finally relaxed and chuckled at Sarah's optimism, conceding, "Just another night at Toro's. My apologies, Bill, I'm sure she was safe with you."

There was no music coming from inside while they were talking, just the gentle sound of pleasant conversation.

On the porch, the front door opened and the glow from the indoor lights spilled onto the four people below. Coming out the door was Tony Jackson. Tony closed the front door behind him, struck a match, and lit his cigarette, momentarily illuminating his face before leaving only the orange tip glowing in the shadow. A minute went by and he opened the door again to throw light on the four people below him, double-checking. Sarah walked to the foot of the stairs and looked up at him with a smile. Sarah's face was arguably the most recognizable face in the world. He stepped to the edge of the porch, and confirmed his original impression: "Sarah Bernhardt? No way."

"Yes, it's me," Sarah answered, and made a guess. "Tony Jackson?"

"Yes ma'am," stuttered the befuddled twenty-six-year-old Professor.

"We came to hear you play, Tony."

"I am truly honored, Miss Sarah." Tony squinted to see who she was with.

"Tony, let me introduce you to my companions." Tony stepped down the staircase and they were now standing together, under the bay window.

"This is my dear friend Bill Farnum."

Bill stepped forward, greeting Tony with a handshake. "Pleased to meet you, Tony."

"The pleasure is mine," Tony replied.

"And this fine young man sitting above us in the cab is our dear friend, Stalebread Lacoume."

Tony walked over to the cab and greeted Stalebread. "I remember seeing your band play when you were kids. I really liked your homemade instruments."

He reached up to take Stalebread's hand. "Let me help you down. I want you to come inside and be my guests. Miss Lulu will be thrilled to have you. She adores you, Miss Sarah. She is your biggest fan, as you will see." Stalebread accepted Tony's offer, and with James' help, he climbed down out of his carriage. Tony was tickled to be meeting the local legend Stalebread. He told him, "My first instrument was homemade. It was no toy, either! Hey, you kids weren't playing toys. I know."

Stalebread was feeling honored, and tipped his hat out of respect.

Tony continued, "My first instrument was a home-made harpsichord. People threw junk over our backyard fence, at the corner of Amelia Street and Tchoupitoulas. It took a long while to collect what it took to build it, but eventually I had all the parts to complete my harpsichord. Took me quite a while to build, but it worked and I taught myself to play it real well too. 'How Sweet To Have A Home In Heaven' was the first song I played on it. Had my first concert performance right there in our backyard. My mother and my aunties were my audience."

Stalebread confided to Tony, "You know, my boys an' me used to park ourselves under this parlor window when-ever we found out you were playing. This isn't the first time I been parked here, just never so elegantly as up in the cab."

"Well, let's all go inside," Tony suggested while he led the way. "Miss Lulu will be wondering where I am. She doesn't like long breaks being taken by me or her girls." While Tony walked Stalebread up the stairs, he told him more about his homemade harpsichord.

Bill took Sarah's arm and they followed Tony and Stalebread up the stairs. A dark-skinned doorman in a red uniform ushered the four of them inside. He only stood forty inches tall. With his head tipped back, he carefully examined every guest. After the group entered the foyer, Tony said of the stoic concierge, "This is General Jack

Johnson." General Jack nodded, closed the door and resumed his station with a dour expression.

Tony requested of his three guests that they wait in the foyer until he came back with Lulu. "Lulu's going to have a stroke when she sees you, Miss Sarah!" He slipped out of sight down the hallway. General Jack Johnson ignored the new arrivals. He was as still as the palm in the vase he stood next to. The General broke his pose only when a small pack of gallivanting sports passed in front of Mahogany Hall. He leaned into the keyhole below the doorhandle. The General was a bulldog, ready for anything. That was his redeeming trait.

Sarah and Bill admired the huge tapestry that hung on the wall. Its erotic motif featured couples in Hindu Kama Sutra poses. "Some of those positions look like they could hurt," Sarah joked.

"Beautifully arabesque," Bill commented poetically.

Stalebread spoke up. "It smells wonderful in here with all the gardenias."

"They are everywhere!" Sarah exclaimed.

"Gardenias are my favorite flower," Stalebread said. "Intoxicating."

Sarah concurred, "They're mine, too."

"What's the lay of the land, Bill?" Stalebread asked his companion.

"Well, the front door is at our back, and this risqué tapestry that we've been admiring hangs before us. To our left is the parlor," Bill continued. "I only count two couples resting in alcoves at the far side—two old men with two girls."

"It must be a slow night," Sarah interjected, "or maybe

all the inhabitants of Mahogany Hall are upstairs in those rooms right now."

As the three stepped in a little further, Bill continued painting the picture for his sightless friend: "Now, in front of us is the narrow hallway Tony just went down. We're in the foyer, with the staircase leading to the two top floors. I count eight doors on each floor."

A door opened on the top floor and out stepped one of the working girls, wearing little. She leaned on the railing, looked down at the new arrivals, and smiled. Sarah and Bill looked up at the young woman, and smiled back.

At the end of the hallway, Tony reappeared with Madame Lulu White in tow. She paused to check her appearance at a three-quarter length mirror. Lulu tucked a couple of dangling curls back into her coif. She always wanted everything in place: false eyelashes, lipstick, rouge, and hair. Sarah's natural light-red hair was beautiful; long, soft and curly. It was nothing like Lulu's outrageous red wig. Two long, diamond-encrusted hair pins held Lulu's bun in place. After her self-inspection, she caught up with Tony in the foyer and was instantly shocked at the sight of her celebrated guest. "Excuse me but, I must be dreaming." Poor Lulu looked confused and discombobulated. "Is it really you, Miss Bernhardt? I can't believe my eyes!" She looked to Tony in disbelief. "You should have told me, Tony."

"Would you have believed me?"

Lulu said to her guests, "I would not have believed him. Oh, excuse me, please. I'm feeling a little lightheaded."

Madam Lulu White

Sarah gently took Lulu's hand, and assured her, "You are fine, dear. This happens. It will pass. Thank you for receiving us. We came to hear Tony play, if that is all right with you?"

"By all means!" Lulu insisted.

LuLu White and the foyer of Mahogany Hall.

Lulu turned to Bill, whom she also recognized. "William Farnum, why, you are more handsome in person than your pictures. It is a pleasure to meet you. You are for real, too, aren't you—or is this all a dream?"

Bill laughed. "Yes, in the flesh. It is so nice to meet you Lulu. Please, call me Bill."

"All right, Bill," Lulu obliged. "I can't believe I have you two standing here in front of me," she said, still shaking her head. "You have come at a nice quiet time, actually. Just an hour ago I was hosting two dozen members of a fraternal organization." She smiled and added, "I won't say who—I'm no tattletale. At any rate, it was a randy bunch. They were here for three hours. Pierre and I just got through cleaning up after them. I hope no one else shows up tonight. I'm not expecting any more groups anyway, and when it gets later in the evening, the taildraggers never make it this far down the line. They usually find what they can afford in the low-rent cribs, because they can't afford the mansions with what little money they have left at this time of night. There are five clients up there with my girls right now. No, six," Lulu said, gesturing up to the two top floors. "You won't see any of them come down this staircase when they leave. Those six are all married men, I know them all. I have a back staircase they prefer. Married men are like that."

Everyone laughed, including Stalebread. Lulu looked at him and introduced herself.

"Hello, my name is Lulu, I don't think I've had the pleasure."

"No, we've never met, Miss White," Stalebread replied, "but I've been here many times before."

Lulu looked baffled by his cryptic statement and Stalebread hastened to explain. "When we were kids playing music in the District, my band used to play in front of Tom Anderson's. If we caught wind that Tony was playing here, me and my boys would park ourselves under the window in the shadows, just listening to Tony."

"Why, you must be Stalebread Lacoume, then. By golly!" Lulu realized it was true.

"Yes, ma'am," he answered, tipping his boater.

"My, but how you have grown. Well, I'll be. Of course I remember you and your band. That was years and years ago. "

Bill chimed in, "Stalebread and I go way back, too, Lulu. We met when he and his boys used to busk over on Canal Street outside the St. Charles. I was a stock player in the house troupe. The boys used to like their tips in cigarettes. We'd stand around after they played and have a smoke together."

"We all smoked like chimneys back then," Stalebread said. "But I don't smoke that much anymore."

"I've cut way back, too. But I still can't resist a good cigarillo," Sarah admitted.

Lulu's butler gave Lulu the sign that the parlor was ready for them, and she ushered her guests in. The beautiful, spacious room was decorated in Art Nouveau style. Hanging on two separate walls were large, framed Alphonse Mucha lithograph posters depicting Mucha's muse, Sarah Bernhardt, in costume as *Gismonda*, and another poster of her in *La Dame aux Camelias*. Sarah liked seeing Mucha's idealized depictions of her.

"I just love Alphonse," Sarah said to Bill.

"Well, he certainly loves you." The third framed picture of Sarah was a small piece: a monochromatic silverpoint portrait of Sarah in her *Gismonda* costume from around 1896. Sarah whispered to Bill, "That's a study for the *Gismonda* poster."

Tony Jackson sat down at the pearl-white upright piano and Lulu playfully sat down next to him. As he faced the keys, she spun dramatically on the smooth piano bench to face her guests. Queen of her domain, she looked over at the two young women entertaining their clients in the cozy nook. With nothing but her piercing stare, Lulu banished the four of them. The two girls understood and immediately got up to leave. The two men were befuddled by the sudden expulsion, but followed the girls out of the parlor without protest and the four of them ascended the staircase to the second floor.

Mahogany Hall parlor

"Now," Lulu said, watching them disappear, "we have the parlor to ourselves!" Lulu again turned to Tony and now requested he accompany her on "Where the Moon Shines," her favorite song.

As Tony struck up the tune, Sarah, Bill and Stalebread took a seat together on the large sofa in front of the piano. Sarah sat between her companions.

Where the moon shines
The streets are damp and cold
Where the moon shines
Dreams are bought and sold
Under the blue lights flood
Secrets are never told…

Someday soon I know I'm gonna
    leave here
Leave my life to die
Someday I'll be walking
In the sweet by and by
Where the moon shines
So far away from home
Where the moon shines
Everyone is alone
The boulevards and avenues
And no place to atone
Someday soon I know I'm gonna
    go there
Leave my life to die
Someday I'll be walking
In the sweet by and by

When Lulu finished, Sarah, Bill and Stalebread gave her a warm round of applause. Their hostess stood up at the end of the song and left the bench to Tony. Standing in her fabulous black dress, she said to her guests, "Let me go see where Pierre is keeping himself. We need refreshments!"

While Lulu was off with Pierre, Tony entertained

Sarah, Bill and Stalebread with Gottschalk's "Tournament Galop." This was followed by the popular song "Ida," with everyone chiming in on the line, "Sweet as apple cida!"

Tony kept his cut-crystal tip jar beside him on the Chippendale end table. A Tiffany table lamp sat next to the jar and cast its warm light onto Tony's hands, the piano keys, and the tip jar. Only two denominations ever nested in that jar: twenties and hundreds. Some nights there were more of the latter, when big spenders were one-upping each other. The tip jar was stuffed with twenties left by the previous party.

Lulu and Pierre returned to the parlor and distributed flutes of champagne to the guests. Tony nodded when Pierre placed his fluted glass on the end table next to him, and indicated to Pierre that his whiskey glass had run low. Tony liked to keep his tumbler full.

At the end of "Ida," Tony looked over his shoulder and asked, "Do you have a request, Miss Sarah?"

"That was delightful, Tony," Sarah answered, "but perhaps just a wee dose of melancholy to balance such glee?"

Tony pondered this for a moment and asked her, "Do you know the composition by Gottschalk called 'Morte'?"

"Oh, I do!" she said, adding the English translation, "She is dead!"

Tony began to play the song. It was a beautiful dirge, and he executed it with all due pathos while Sarah hummed along in dark harmony. When he had finished the piece, he inquired, "Melancholy enough, Miss Sarah?"

Sarah laughed and conceded, "Perhaps too much

melancholy." An ironic sentiment, coming from the super-star known to repose in her very own plush coffin.

Tony countered, "Well, how about this next one? It's a happy medium, but not too happy. It's a lively number, yet has the morbid distinction of being the song Gottschalk was playing when he died at the piano. Naturally, this fact adds an element of pity. It is called "Tremolo." But I think it is best played four-handed. Do you play piano, Miss Sarah?" Tony asked.

"Oh, heavens," Sarah replied, "I've not played in years, but Stalebread will accompany you in my stead, if you need another set of hands. Stalebread is a wonderful pianist. He played for us earlier tonight."

The Professor was delighted to hear this, though Stale-bread was startled when she volunteered his service. He nearly froze with fear.

"Stalebread, help me out with this one, won't you?"

Sarah rose from the sofa and took Stalebread's hands in hers. Captive in her grip, he was led to the piano. Bill chuckled, "I told you so, Stalebread. It's impossible to say no to Sarah, isn't it?"

Tony indicated to Sarah that she should seat their recruit on the left end of the bench. Stalebread sat down shoulder-to-shoulder with the great Tony Jackson Jr., terribly nervous.

"Don't worry," Tony assured him, "I'll show you your part. It'll be fun, I promise." Tony leaned over and gave his impromptu accompanist a quick rehearsal. Stalebread fell right into it, and Tony said, "Okay, let's GO!"

They started their rambunctious "Tremolo" with four hands galloping back and forth across the keys, as

Gottschalk had intended. Everyone was knocked out by their three-and-a-half-minute explosion. When the song concluded, Stalebread was left exhausted yet exhilarated. Their small audience rose for a standing ovation.

Stalebread stood up and reached out a hand, expecting to be escorted back to the sofa. "Would you stay and play some more, Stalebread?" asked Tony.

The reluctant accompanist demurred, "Thank you for offering, Tony, but…"

"Oh, just stay here for a song or two before you go back to your sofa. It will still be there when you get back to it," he teased. Stalebread sat back down at the keys.

"Do you know 'Meet Me In St. Louis'?" Tony asked.

"Sure." Stalebread answered.

"How about 'The Good Old Summertime'?"

"Sure. I know both of those."

Tony had chosen a couple tunes he was sure Stalebread knew.

"Perfect! Let's play them back-to-back. Stay with me and we'll dovetail them together."

The two natural-born musicians had a romp with the two songs, and made a smooth transition between the songs seamlessly, like they'd been playing together for years.

Applause rained down as the song was finishing, and Stalebread rose from the piano to signal he was done.

"Thank you so much, Tony. It was such an honor." He added, "I better not overstay my welcome. Mom always says, 'Don't cut the branch you're sitting on.'"

Tony chuckled. "We should all heed your mother's wisdom."

Sarah took Stalebread by the hand and led him back to his spot on the sofa.

Tony called over to Lulu, who stood with Pierre in the threshold of the foyer. "Miss Lulu, I do believe we have ourselves a future Professor with Stalebread here." Tony's comment was music to Stalebread's ears.

General Jack approached Lulu, who bent down to hear what he had to say. Beaming with approval, Lulu followed behind the General to the front door. He opened it for her. She stepped outside for a moment and returned, escorting a slender Creole lad who looked to be in his early teens. Lulu turned to her guests and introduced him by name. "Friends, please welcome Tony's young protégé, Ferdinand La Menthe. Or, as he calls himself these days, 'Winding Boy.'"

Tony, with a sweeping gesture, invited Ferdinand (who would later become famous under the moniker "Jelly Roll" Morton) to come to the piano. He winked at Sarah, Bill, and Stalebread, knowing they were in for a treat.

Ferdinand jumped at the offer. Tony relinquished the bench to Winding Boy. Without bothering to announce the songs, the youth played a dazzling medley of Scott Joplin's ragtime hits, all mixed up in a jumble.

Stalebread was quite impressed by Winding Boy and whispered to Bill and Sarah, "He's the real deal."

After ten minutes or so of tickling the ivories, the young lion stood and stretched his arms toward the ceiling. Everyone in the room then rose for an intermission. Tony stood at Ferdinand's side, telling him, "Winding Boy, you sure got Joplin down."

The guests mingled and stretched, walking around the

parlor and taking in curiosities. Stalebread remained on the sofa, still basking in Tony Jackson's approval. Sarah and Bill admired the white cockatiel sleeping in its gilded cage. The cockatiel opened its eyes, and began speaking, "Where's the cat?" The cockatiel repeated the one-liner over and over. "Where's the cat? Where's the cat?" That had all the guests laughing.

22. JOHN THE BAPTIST

John was the first Professor I had when I opened Mahogany Hall.
—Lulu White

DURING THE INTERMISSION, PIERRE CAME BACK INTO the parlor and whispered to Lulu. She was comforting her pet squirrel monkey, Napoleon, who was tethered to his bejeweled collar. The proprietor and her pet listened intently to Pierre.

"I know it's late," Lulu announced to her guests, "but we have one last arrival. I shall return momentarily. To celebrate this auspicious moment, I'd like to bring out my favorite year of Moët Chandon." With that, she left the parlor, with Napoleon leading her down the long hallway toward the back door. Pierre popped another bottle of champagne.

Waiting inside the back entrance by the laundry room was a tawny gentleman with wavy white hair and a Caribbean air, dressed in a caramel-colored suit, a gold brocade vest, and a brown string tie. All were accentuated by a flawless white shirt with ruffled cuffs secured by gold-nugget cufflinks. The elderly gentleman fidgeted with his riverboat gambler's hat. He had beautiful hands.

Lulu wistfully greeted her dear friend. "John, John, John the Baptist, thank you for coming on such short notice."

Her guest impishly wagged his long fingers toward heaven, replying, "In this marvelous modern age of electricity, all things are possible."

Lulu agreed and added, "Luckily you were at your sister's house, because that's the only telephone number I had."

He replied, "Glad you tracked me down, Miss Lulu. When Violet came running down to the dock I was just about to shove off for Delacroix."

Lulu explained her reason for summoning him. "Creditors are closing in on me, John. I have to skedaddle for a while. I am locking up Mahogany Hall in the morning and taking the noon train to Los Angeles. But just for a spell."

"Why Los Angeles?" John asked.

"I'm building a movie studio in Hollywood. I want to see what my man George Kilshaw has found for me. You remember George."

"You're still with that grifter?"

"Yeah—can't seem to shake him, John. Well, anyway, I sent him out a month ago to scout properties. Seems like a great place to make movies, perfect weather year-round. I fancy myself getting behind the camera, and directing. After all, can't be much different than what I do here, wouldn't you say? By the way, did you bring along some of your John the Conqueror Root? I need it for my trip."

The old man said, "Yes. I certainly did. Violet told me to bring some for you. I brought a piece I found inside Devil's Punchbowl. It's got strong juju. Now I see why you requested some, seeing as this root will give you a leg up on any new business ventures."

John reached into his pocket and pulled out a small bulbous root with two short shoots. As he handed it over, he reminded her, "Now, before any kind of business meeting, or in a court of law, take a bite off one of those shoots, chew it, then spit it out. Not into a cuspidor, mind you—it's got to hit the ground. And that ain't all the John the Conqueror Root can do. I'll remind you. It can keep your spirits up during times of trials and tribulations."

Lulu tucked the John the Conqueror Root into her bustle.

"Thank you so much, John. Now there is one other favor I'll ask of you, which is really what made me think of tracking you down in the first place. Since tonight is my big 'pretend' last night in Mahogany Hall, I wanted you to come and play the Pearl. It's been ten years since I opened this place, and you were the very first one to play her. I thought, if I could get you, it would be an auspicious way to close up shop, even though it is just going to be temporary. And here you are."

John smiled. "And here I am!"

She took John the Baptist by the arm, and they walked side-by-side down the hallway toward the foyer with Napoleon scurrying along, leading the way.

"We have a distinguished guest in the parlor who

would *love* to hear you play," Lulu said in a hushed tone. "It's none other than Sarah Bernhardt."

"*The* Sarah Bernhardt?"

"Yes. *The* Sarah Bernhardt!"

"My, oh my," sighed John.

Lulu added, "She's here with William Farnum, the actor, and Stalebread Lacoume."

As they stepped into the foyer, John the Baptist saw General Jack over at his post. The two old acquaintances gave each other a nod of recognition. John said under his breath to Lulu, "Still got that little devil working for you, I see."

Lulu answered him in a whisper, "I had to send him to Countess Willie a couple of months ago, after he bit one of my customers. About a month ago she sent him back to me, because he threatened one of her customers with his brass knuckles."

Lulu and John stepped into the parlor, where Tony immediately recognized John the Baptist. He trembled at the sight of his idol, whom he hadn't seen in nearly a decade. Lulu pointed to Tony, sitting at the piano. "See, Tony Jackson is here tonight. too."

Every eye in the room turned to the threshold and fell on John. John the Baptist spoke across the room to Tony. "It does my heart good to see you after all these years, Tony." John addressed everyone present when he looked at Tony and exclaimed, "Orpheus incarnate!"

Lulu singled out Ferdinand: "John, this is Tony's sixteen-year-old protégé, Ferdinand La Menthe. 'Winding Boy,' as he likes to call himself. He just played a wonderful set of Joplin for us."

John tipped his hat, saying, "Pleased to meet you, Winding Boy."

Ferdinand replied, "The honor is mine."

Lulu turned John's attention toward the sofa occupied by Bill on the left, Stalebread on the right, and Sarah in the middle. Sarah hardly needed an introduction, with the two large Alphonse Mucha posters of her image hanging on the wall right behind her. John the Baptist bowed to Sarah in a gentlemanly manner, and she stood up and curtsied, like a young girl. Lulu introduced Bill: "William Farnum, the actor."

Bill stood up and shook John's hand. He did not recognize the man, but graciously responded, "How do you do, Mr. Farnum?"

John was introduced to the person wearing sunglasses. "Last, but not least," Lulu said, "we have Stalebread Lacoume." Stalebread stood up to meet John face-to-face. With his left hand he removed his sunglasses to reveal his blindness. His right hand reached out to grasp John's. After they shook hands, John responded to Lulu's introduction, "Stalebread, now, there's a name I have not heard in a very long time. I used to take the five o'clock ferry from Algiers. I used to see your spasm band years ago at the foot of Canal Street, playing for the commuters on their way home to Algiers."

"Stalebread plays piano these days," Lulu updated John.

John said, "Nice to see you again after all these years."

Stalebread agreed. "Nice to see you, too. It has been a long time."

In the foyer, General Jack manned the front door,

motionless as an old toad, but when he heard footsteps coming up the stairs he looked through the keyhole and opened the door before the doorbell could be rung. The General went outside and talked to someone on the porch, then admitted a young sport not yet out of his teens. Everyone turned to see who was last to arrive.

This latest guest slid into the parlor, keeping his eyes down and his body hunched low so as not to interrupt the proceedings.

Lulu whispered to John the Baptist, "Kid Ross. He always shows up when Tony's here. He's uncanny that way. Learns all he can from Tony."

As he slipped past them, John looked Kid Ross over and asked Lulu skeptically, "Is he any good?"

Lulu replied, "I hear tell he can play. You know, I've never invited him to play the Pearl. Tony says he's good and getting better but, as far as I'm concerned, just 'good' isn't good enough to play the Pearl. He sure is wily about showing up whenever Tony's here. He used to park himself under the window just to listen to Tony, like people sometimes do. He's a good kid, so I finally gave him permission to come on in."

Kid Ross sat in a chair next to the sofa where Stalebread sat.

Tony took a gulp of his whiskey and resumed playing. He was extremely self-conscious in front of John the Baptist but announced, "I think I will try out a new song I've been working on. I call it 'Don't Leave Me in the Ice and Snow.'" Winding Boy sat next to him on an ottoman, listening intently. Everyone focused on the performance.

At the conclusion of "Ice and Snow," the room filled with applause.

"I'm glad that meets with your approval. I think I'll try another new one out on you. I call this one, 'I'll Certny See About That.'"

Staring over at John the Baptist, Kid Ross whispered to Stalebread, "Who's the old man?"

"John the Baptist, Lulu's original Professor," Stalebread whispered back.

Kid Ross got wide-eyed. "Well, I'll be damned, I heard he got killed, up in Natchez Under-the-Hill." Stalebread shushed him.

Tony finished his song "I'll Certny See About That." Still nervous in the presence of his idol, Tony stuttered as he asked John the Baptist to play for them, rising from the bench and beckoning John the Baptist to take his seat at the Pearl.

As John the Baptist came over to the piano with solemn reverence, Lulu announced, "This is an auspicious occasion to have John the Baptist here tonight. John was the first Professor I had when I opened Mahogany Hall ten years ago. He was playing for Queen Gertie at the time. I was lucky to steal our Prince away from the Queen and get away with it! Oh, she was red hot mad about it, too, let me tell you. Me and her met outside one day and Gertie slapped me with a white glove. She was holding a pepper box in her other hand, so I buried my hat pin in her thigh and relieved her of her pistol. I can tell you, John the Baptist was worth fighting for. When he came over to Mahogany Hall I took out a full-page ad in the *Blue Book* announcing his arrival. That got old Queen

Gertie spittin' mad, but she never came back for more of my hat pins."

Everyone laughed as Lulu continued, "I heard the other day from Pierre that John was in Algiers at his sister Violet's. I was so happy when I tracked him down. I asked him to come over and play for us tonight. You see, I'm leaving for Los Angeles tomorrow, and, well, I've decided to board up Mahogany Hall before I leave. I might be gone for just a little while, but I'm telling you, it won't be long before I'm back. You'll read about it in all the newspapers—that Mahogany Hall has gone out of business, that I've run off and lost Mahogany Hall. Well, you are hearing it straight from the horse's mouth: I am not losing this place. I'll be gone, but I'll be back. I've got to go on the lam until I shake off my most persistent creditors. I have to take the train out to Hollywood tomorrow. You heard it here first from me. It will be written up in the morning newspapers that Mahogany Hall is shut for good. That's the word I want out there. So, to complete the illusion, my farewell soiree tonight is a swan song, and who better to grace the Pearl on this pretend last night? Ladies and gentlemen, I give you John the Baptist!"

After Lulu's grand introduction, John the Baptist ceremoniously removed his hat, handing it off to Pierre. Lulu helped relieve John of his suitcoat, and gave that to Pierre, too. John the Baptist nodded to each of the guests before being seated at his beloved piano.

"I love the Pearl," he said as he leaned over and kissed the piano.

John the Baptist began his concert with his amazing rendition of Louis Gottschalk's "Bamboula," a full ten minutes long. The Original Professor followed this with his beautiful rendition of "La Paloma," weaving many improvisations into the tune. The song carried everyone on its wings until John the Baptist glided it all to a halt with one long, last sustained note.

Acknowledging superstar Sarah among the guests, John asked her for a song. Squeezing Stalebread's arm, she suggested "Over the Waves." Unable to resist the rousing melody, all the guests began humming along.

When John's song faded into pure noodling, Pierre came back into the parlor with a large silver tray. This immediately caught John the Baptist's eye and made him smile. On the tray stood a dusty bottle of absinthe, and a crystal pitcher of ice water with cubes bobbing at the top. Next to the set-up was a small crystal bowl full of sugar cubes, accompanied by sterling silver tongs. A crystal cocktail snifter and a sterling-silver slotted spoon completed the array.

Pierre put the tray on the Chippendale end table to John's right. The Professor told the gathering, "I've been gone for years, but they still have my private bottle. That's what I call home!" Pierre smiled as he carefully wiped the dust off the entire bottle with the white serviette that had been draped over his forearm. John slid closer to the tray. The bottle had a label with a risqué wood nymph chasing a wafting mist. John removed the cork and took a long sniff. The old Professor turned to his audience and showed them his prize.

"It is still unopened," John said as he swirled the cloudy green liquid. "This is my favorite brand of absinthe." He looked over at Pierre. "We will be needing more snifters, Pierre, and more slotted spoons!" John's eyes crossed the room, taking a headcount: Tony, Ferdinand, Bill, Stalebread, Sarah, and Kid Ross. He looked further back and included Lulu. "Pierre, my good man, we will be needing seven more snifters."

Pierre quickly returned with a tray of more snifters and put it on the table. Like a true alchemist, John the Baptist began his mixology with mystical decorum. First, the Professor filled each snifter half-full of ice water, then placed a slotted spoon across the rim of each snifter. With the tongs, the maestro placed a sugar cube onto each slotted spoon that John had rested on the rim of each glass. The prepared vessels stood ready as John slowly baptized each sugar cube with a copious shot of absinthe. The green fluid dripped through the slotted spoons. When it mixed with the ice water below, smoky wisps rose, and the ice water turned a milky chartreuse. John pivoted on the bench to face everyone. "I propose a toast!" The mixologist nodded to Pierre to distribute the drinks. Pierre removed the slotted spoons and the chartreuse liquid swirled around in the snifters as they were handed out.

John the Baptist began his toast. "To my dear friend, Miss Lulu. May your flight be protected by your guardian angel, your John the Conqueror root, and your hatpin." Everyone laughed as John went on. "And may your absence from Mahogany Hall be short-lived. You will be missed in the meantime. Here's to more absinthe and less absence!"

"Hear, hear!" the guests chimed in. The revered Professor continued his benediction. "Friends, raise your glasses with me. À vôtre santé!" John the Baptist's voice rang out.

The participants joined in the toast, "À vôtre santé!"

Stalebread held his drink cautiously, like it was nitro-glycerin, for he had heard the stories of insanity attributed to absinthe intoxication. When Stalebread slowly sipped the concoction he was pleasantly surprised. The neophyte savored the anise flavor, and finished his drink.

John the Baptist soon felt the effects of the absinthe and began tickling the Pearl's keys once again, commencing in a slow, dreamy way, but with the cadence of a tango. It captured his audience, who were also feeling the effects of John the Baptist's favorite absinthe. His improvised composition took flight, and his listeners were his passengers. They rose up in spirit to the ceiling and were lit like the chandelier. This composition seemed time-less to all who imbibed in the absinthe. In real time, it lasted the length of a classical suite, with many different pieces woven together. A dreamscape enveloped the room. It was as if clouds and sky had replaced the plaster ceiling in the parlor. When John the Baptist brought them back down to earth, he came out of his trance, noodling on the keys while he regained his consciousness.

John the Baptist confided to Tony, Ferdinand, and Stalebread, "I am very content in my long life. I would like to hear what makes my fellow ivory-ticklers content. Tony," said John, "we'll start with you. Tell me what your innermost wish is. What would make you content?"

Tony had been drinking steadily and the absinthe further loosened his mind. He answered old John, speaking directly to him. "John, I do believe I will be content when I finally get up to Chicago."

John the Baptist leaned in to hear Tony's answer and a nervous Tony blurted out a foolish giggle. John looked back at him crossly.

Tony apologetically addressed John the Baptist again, trying to explain, "You see, I have a sister and cousins up there. I have many loved ones in Chicago and they all tell me I will take that town by storm after I get there. Now see, here's the thing; I don't like the thought of leaving my mother down there on Amelia Street, and I don't like the thought of leaving New Orleans. It hurts me to even think about it, honestly. However, you know, Chicago just sounds awfully good to me. I really and truly do think Chicago will make me content."

John listened closely and pronounced his admonition in verse.

> Chicago won't be warm like New
> Orleans.
> Chicago will chill you out in the
> cold.
> You'll get warm from the flame of
> the fame, but that flame of
> fame will burn you.
> You will end up burning your
> candle from both ends just to
> stay warm.

Tony laughed despite there being nothing funny to

laugh at. John scolded him. "Take this warning seriously, Tony. It's not a laughing matter! I'm trying to warn you."

Tony apologized, his eyes downcast.

John the Baptist had no more to say to Tony, so he moved on to Ferdinand. While continuing to play, John posed the same question to Ferdinand, who was feeling even cockier than his usual cocky self, due to the absinthe. The sixteen-year-old was ready for the old man's query and he stood up, thumbs hooked on his suspenders, a broad smile on his face. "I want to conquer the world!" he said, looking from side to side to see if he made the desired impression. Kid Ross and Stalebread were quite impressed by Winding Boy's lofty ambition and self-confidence, which neither of them possessed.

"Winding Boy," John said, "you will travel the world. It will be your oyster and it will be served up on a black lacquer plate. You will get your wish."

Ferdinand beamed with pride when he heard this, and he sat back down in his chair quite content with the maestro's prediction.

John cocked his head and after a pause added, "For a while." He concluded with a bit of advice. "Young man, you would benefit from a little humility."

Winding Boy looked perplexed but overall pleased with John the Baptist's prophecy. He replied in earnest, "I'll look into that. Maybe I can get some of that humility somehow."

Next in line for the sage's inquisition was Stalebread. Kid Ross leaned over and whispered, "You're next up, Stalebread." Stalebread finished his last drop of absinthe. In a dreamy state, he nodded that he was ready for his turn. He waited patiently, knowing the questioning would begin when John resumed playing the piano.

John the Baptist's fingers meandered over the keys and he began, "Stalebread, I don't need to ask you. You have always been content. You've always been content with who you are and where you're at." Stalebread thought about what he'd been told and nodded, knowing it was true.

Stalebread pondered a fact he had always known but never thought about. He asked John, "How do I manage to stay content? Can you tell me that?"

"You have the heart of a child. Always have had that. Just don't lose it."

"Thank you, John." Stalebread was content with John's reply.

Kid Ross leaned over to Stalebread. "You lucky!"

Both Sarah and Bill were falling asleep on the sofa. Their eyes were closed, but they were both listening and smiling.

Winding Boy looked Stalebread over, up and down. He had never heard that term "the heart of a child" and he had no clue what it meant. Lulu knew, though. She knew many girls in the business who possessed the heart of a child. Lulu was touched by the sweetness of Old John's assessment of Stalebread.

John the Baptist asked Stalebread, "You don't have any ambitions to leave New Orleans like Tony and Winding Boy, do you?"

"None," Stalebread declared.

"I didn't think so," said John.

Stalebread thought for a moment and spoke of his true ambitions: "I won't ever leave New Orleans, but I do have some mighty strong ambitions. I'm going to build a house and have a family. That's what I dream of."

John the Baptist smiled at Stalebread's heartfelt conviction and stopped playing the Pearl. The questioning ceased and the people in the room fell quiet. A calm dreamy state took over and time seemed to stand still. The guests had fallen under the influence of the absinthe, the "green fairy."

Eventually, Stalebread gently stood up, leaving the sleepy Sarah and Bill on the sofa. They stirred and opened their eyes to see him standing above them. Stalebread leaned down and told them it was time for him to head home.

"I'll see you both tomorrow night at The Tulane. My mother said she'd go with me. She'll be thrilled to meet all y'all."

Sarah said, "Olga's opening night will be fantastique!"

Stalebread yawned. "It surely will be, but for now, I need to get some sleep!"

Sarah and Bill slowly stood.

"I need to get to bed, too!" Sarah agreed.

Bill pointed out the window. "Look Sarah, the moon is setting! We really should get going."

"It has truly been a pleasure," Stalebread said to everyone in the room. "Thank you, one and all, for a magical night." Pierre came to Stalebread's side, and guided him out of the parlor.

In the foyer, Lulu and Tony stood near the front door to say goodbye to Stalebread. Tony took Stalebread's right hand, saying, "We'll have to play together again sometime.

Whenever I get back from Chicago. I won't be there forever, according to John."

Stalebread replied, "You take care of yourself, Tony. I'll still be here in New Orleans when you get back. We'll play together again, I promise. Someday I'll tell my grandchildren that I played with the great Tony Jackson!"

Tony blushed.

Lulu stepped up to hug Stalebread goodbye. "When I return from Los Angeles, I want you to come back to Mahogany Hall and play The Pearl for me, regularly."

"I would love it, too," Stalebread answered. "I won't be able to fill Tony's shoes, but I would appreciate the opportunity. Take care out in California, Lulu. After you open your movie studio, you can hire Sarah and Bill, right?"

"That's just what I'll do!" she said. "Let's hope this new motion-picture craze isn't a flash in the pan." She assured him, "I have my John the Conqueror Root. I'll be fine. Don't you worry, I'll track you down when I get back."

Stalebread handed her his business card and responded, "I'm gonna take you up on your offer, Lulu. Call me whenever you need me."

General Jack held the front door open, and Pierre escorted Stalebread out the door, telling his charge, "There are twelve steps to the sidewalk. I will walk you down to your cab."

The night was coming to an end. The moon dipped into the river fog. Basin Street was now quiet, except for the sound of the junkman's wagon clanking and clattering down the street.

At the bottom of the stairs, Pierre walked Stalebread over to James' cab and they woke the cabbie.

"Good morning, James," Stalebread said.

James opened his eyes and greeted him groggily, "Oh, good morning, Mister Stalebread." He got down from his perch and helped his passenger into the cab. "Here's my hand."

Pierre stood by to make sure Stalebread had boarded safely, then said goodbye. Stalebread thanked Pierre for his help.

As James tucked a coachman's blanket around his passenger's lap, he asked, "That's that for tonight, Mr. Stalebread? We could go down to Café Du Monde and get you some coffee and beignets before I take you home, if you'd like."

"No, thank you, James," answered his passenger with a smile. "I really do need some sleep."

"So, that's that?" James replied.

"Yep," Stalebread confirmed. "That's that with that."

In His Own Words

I quote Stalebread from print interviews here, to give some examples of his storytelling voice. There are no known audio interviews.

Stalebread on how he informed his mother of his intention to be the family breadwinner:

I told her, "I want Emma and Jimmy to have the education we never had."

Stalebread on forming his band:

We began with that old piece, "Georgia Camp Meeting." I had an awful time training 'em. But we'd been whistlin' the stuff like "Rosie O'Grady" and pretty soon I had 'em like a well-oiled machine. All those slinky slides and hesitations, and the bang-bang stuff, and the sudden stops. I worked 'em all out in my head and drilled my gang.

Stalebread on visiting the Newsboys' Home at suppertime:

Dog-gone! Them were the days, Old Mother Kelly serving her stew and beans and bread for twenty cents.

Stalebread taught banjo, guitar, and piano

Stalebread's star pupils included world-famous magician Blackstone

Stalebread, to a journalist, on the band's public debut:

Our first band performance was on Royal Street between Canal and Iberville. We cut loose! Boy, they didn't know what they were hearing... but they sure liked it! Say, we had that street blocked within five minutes! The Royal Street sports filled our hat with coins when we passed it around. They knew their band had arrived. Then and there, Stalebread's band was on the job!

Stalebread on his "war story":

Then things began to happen. Did you know I was a veteran of the First War with Germany? Sure. There were these dinky German bands playing on the streets of New Orleans then. We'd trail 'em. One of 'em would start playing something like "Dixie." We'd be camped on the other side of the street. Just when they'd get started, Whang bam! We'd start into it with some hot jazz, though we didn't know what to call it then. And when we began to cut into their coin, there was some hot battles in Exchange Alley, and Royal Street and even on Canal Street.

Stalebread on their historic two-stop tour:

We went on the road. We got as far as Shreveport and there, the first jazz band in the world was stranded for the first time. We played on the streets and passed the hat making enough for coffee and cakes, and enough to get us to Jackson, Mississippi.

Stalebread on their courtroom appearance:

They brought us up in the Second Recorder's Court. "Who's the leader of this gang?" he asks. I steps-up and confesses, "It's me." "You are charged with disturbing the peace, blocking traffic, public nuisance among other things," he says. "We're not a Public Nuisance. We're a band, Your Honor," I tells him. He ponders for a few moments and then breaks his silence. "If you are a band, let's hear you play."

Stalebread on first meeting Olga at the Tulane Theater:

We all went in as a bunch. At the end of the first act she came out for a curtain call, and I threw her a big bouquet over the footlights. She smiled and bowed and threw me a kiss. She then leaned forward and started to pick it up. I had tied a fishing line to the bouquet and I pulled it. She chased that bouquet halfway across the stage. The audience was howling before she gave up. We ought to have waited to the last act, because the management bounced us. Gave us the bum's rush out on the street.

Newspaper illustration of Stalebread

Well, we went around and waited at the stage door, and when she came out we started playing for her, and that amused her. Then she invited the whole band to come and visit her at her hotel. We did.

She told me that she was going to send me to school. She fixed it up before she left town, for me to go to Miss Sophie Wright's and that's where I got my education.

A story about Stalebread in the *New Orleans States*, 1923

ABOUT MICHAEL SHURTZ

Michael Shurtz is an artist and a writer who resides in Boulder, Colorado. He was personally asked to write Stalebread and the Razzy Dazzy Band by Stalebread's only daughter Rose Lacoume Weaver. His research on the subject dates back to 1988 and this book was ten years in the making. Shurtz' published a book of New Orleans centric short stories MOJOS volume one in 2000, and is currently working on his upcoming book titled *The White Witch and the Saxons.*

At the start of his artistic career, Shurtz was employed by Hanna-Barbera Studios as an 'inbetweener' drawing Saturday Morning cartoons. Later he became the first editorial cartoonist for Billboard Magazine, and went on to design posters for Bill Graham's Fillmore Auditorium.